MW00641573

First Printing, 2023

The Blood Of Royals

Written & Illustrated

by

Christopher Sheen Aldridge

Contents

Contents

Contents

Introduction

Through the generations of vampire lore and the multitude of stories derived from it. I have always yearned for a story that took us to the beginning. A story that shows us a time that has been washed away by lies. A story that tells the true past before it was diluted by those who want us to forget.

My story follows the life of Lord Jackson during a time when Lords, Ladies, Princes, Princesses, Kings, and Queens where all born of royal vampire blood. It was a time where they coexisted with humans who lived as peasants. Peasants who lived to provide nourishment to their Vampire rulers and guardians, and ones they sometimes considered friends.

When Lord Jackson and his crew find out there is a plague devastating the humans turning them into flesh eating zombies they must fight together with the humans to save their food source. History books now call this time the first black plague. A shallow and poor attempt to cover up the truth. A way to keep the wool pulled down over humanities eyes, but I know the truth. I know what happened and I want nothing more than to share it with you.

With countless hours of research and anonymous testimonies from those who were there yet still unwilling to give up their true Identities. I bring to you this story in hopes it will paint a truth of how vampires truly lived not so long ago. In hopes it brings more insight as to how it all began and where it will all be heading.

With that said I want to thank all of those who have shown support throughout the years. The people out there who have pushed me and encouraged me to never stop. Even when the world tried to silence me, the truth, and discoveries that have come to light making this story what it is today.

Thank you all.

A cold smoke rose thru the ashes of the mansion he once called home. The explosion was heard from quite a distance. Flaming rubble and glass where scattered across the grounds. At the end of the driveway he sat on his motorcycle, a 1953 Harley Panhead he had restored back in the 70's and kept stored away for just this very moment. He glimpsed to see the destruction from his rear view mirror, he revved his engine and began to ride down the street. Without a second glace or even a thought, his old life was over and his next inevitable chapter was about to take heed.

Change doesn't happen overnight but you need to keep pushing forward. The cool air, as he rode through the night, flowed thru his long brown hair causing more and more loose strands to fly free from the hair band that attempted to keep it all together. His white t-shirt was plastered to his chest and his robe started to flap in the air. The faster he rode the more it resembled a super hero's cape in the wind as he flew thru the air. Truth be told, that was as close to feeling like a super hero he had felt in a long time. So he kept on riding. Faster and faster he went trying to keep his focus on the cool breeze ahead.

After riding for hours with no direction and no intent as to where he was headed, he began to realize he may not be as prepared for this trip as he would have liked. He also realized that his current attire may not be suitable for the occasion and, therefore he may need to acquire something more substantial.

As the dawn drew near, he reached the town of Antioch. Antioch was a very small farming town, the type of town to have more livestock than people. As he rode through the quite little town he saw nothing but farm after farm. Then as he passed one of the farms he noticed a farmer not much bigger than himself start to get into a pickup truck. Thinking on his feet he decided to ride up ahead a ways, and then circle back to the farm and see if the farmer's truck was still there. As he got closer to the farm he saw that the truck was gone. Figuring he has nothing to lose he pulled up to the house got off his bike walked up to the front door and knocked. Without hearing a sound he figured the house was empty. So without hesitation he took his bike around back and checked for movement in the windows.

It seemed the coast was clear and as he walked to the backdoor he removed his robe. With it he wrapped up his hand and in one fluid motion he sent his fist straight thru the pane of glass that separated him from the brass knob that unlocked that door. He slowly cracked the door open making sure to listen for any movement, but nothing was heard except for the faint chirping of crickets in the backyard. With an unexpected confidence he proceeded into the house and surveyed the surroundings.

He quickly made his way thru the kitchen, the dining room, and the living room. All of which looked as if a miniature tornado had ran thru. Pizza boxes, liquor bottles, newspapers, even the couch looked as if someone has been sleeping on it for so long there was a permanent imprint of a man's figure imbedded in the cushions. As he found himself in front of a set of stairs just by the front door. He quickly took a peek thru the long window just to the right of the door to see if there was any sign of return from the man he saw leave a few minutes prior. He came to the conclusion that he was still in the clear so he proceeded up the stairs.

Unlike the downstairs, the upstairs was immaculate. It took him no time at all to find the bedroom. He opened the door, and surveyed the room. The bed was beautifully made with a matching light blue flower print comforter and pillow set that looked as if it was just ordered from a catalog. The furniture all matched with a cherry wood finish and a doily neatly placed on each surface. Wedding photos and matching lamps on each nightstand. It looked as if the room hasn't been touched by a human hand in quite some time. He scoured the closet and dressers to find any clothes that would fit. He came across a simple pair of jeans and a black Guns and Roses t-shirt he quickly threw on. Both the shirt and the pants were a size bigger than what he would have liked. Even though they were not the best fit they did the job so he kept it moving. Grabbing a couple more items for the road he then proceeded back downstairs. As he passed back thru the kitchen he grabbed his robe and a garbage bag from an open box on the counter. He shoved the robe and extra clothes in the bag and tied it up.

Getting back to his bike he opened up the side satchel and placed the bag inside. He grabbed the handle bars and in one fluid motion threw his leg over the bike kick starting the engine and took off. Back to the road. Back to the breeze.

A couple of miles down the road he saw a diner. A quaint little hole in the wall with a great big neon sign that read Antioch Diner. He pulls into the gravel parking lot and found a spot near the door. He turned off the bike and took a moment to himself. Realizing he hasn't eaten anything all night and feeling the adrenaline finally subside he decided to go in for a bite to eat. After hopping off the bike he reached into the side satchel and pulled out a brown paper bag. He reached into the bag and pulled out a crisp new fifty dollar bill. The bag was then folded and placed back in the side satchel. He tucked the money nicely into his pocket and he headed to the door.

"Have a seat anywhere you like sweetie" said the waitress pouring water into a coffee machine behind the counter "someone will be right with you".

The Blood of Royals

He sat in a booth by the window that overlooked his bike. He placed his elbows on the table and his forehead to his palms and just eased his eyes shut. Not to sleep but, to calm the pounding that was forming in his head. He felt something brush his forearm. Realizing it was the menu he took his finger and pinned the menu to the table. Without even looking up he orders. “Coffee, black, two eggs, over easy, bacon... and toast” then released his finger from the menu allowing the waitress to take it away. He then placed his palm back to his forehead.

His coffee, along with a small plate containing two aspirins, and a glass of water was laid out in front of him. He looked up to thank the kind soul who had the foresight to help ease the pounding in his head, and was stopped dead in his tracks to see a face he has not seen in quite some time. Not quite sure the face in front of him was actually who he believed it to be, he asked “Sarah?”

“No,” in a sweet southern twang she replied “I'm Katie”.

“Sorry, I'm Jack. You just look a lot like someone I haven't seen in a while. Thank you for this.” He said as he picked up the aspirin and tossed them into his mouth. “You looked like you could use it” she said with a smile “Your food will be right up”.

As she turned to help another table he noticed a big scar on her right calf muscle. Well, I guess that couldn't be her, he thought to himself with a chuckle. He placed his forehead back into his palms and eased his eyes close.

A couple minutes went by and Katie dropped off his food. “Enjoy.” she said with a wink and a smile. “I will…” he started to say as he was rudely interrupted by an older man in a cheap suite.

“Katie, I need to see you in the back. Now!” ordered the man as he held the kitchen door open till Katie walked thru. The man’s eyes noticeably lowered toward her rear as he followed behind.

As Jack finished his meal he folded up the last bit of his toast using it to soak up the little bit of yolk left on his plate. He leaned back in the booth feeling calm and satisfied. He savored the last bite as he placed it gently in his mouth. He took a look around the diner to see were Katie was so he could ask her for the check, but she was nowhere to be seen. He figured she was probably still in the back so he calmly waited for her to return.

Five minutes passed and she finally came out from the back. She grabbed the pot of coffee and walked to the few tables that had people in them to refill there cups. As she reached Jacks table he realized her cheery disposition was replaced by a big red mark along the side of her face and her hands were noticeably shaking as she poured coffee into his cup. She couldn’t bring herself to look anybody in the eyes. So he had a pretty good indication of what had happened. He gently grabbed her by the wrist as she put down the coffee pot and he placed a fifty dollar bill into her hand. “Thank you for everything,” he said as he stood up to leave.

“Wait,” she said as she stopped him “This is way too much. I can’t accept this.” She held out the money to give it back. He turned and looked her straight into her eyes. "Trust me, you are worth so much more" and secured it back into her hand. Then he turned, walked out the door, and got back on his bike.

He rode away from the diner till he was no longer in view then slowed. He saw a small dirt path that looked to lead to the back of the diner. He then proceeded to ride around to the back so as not to be seen. He took a moment to compose himself and started to walk to the back door. Conveniently the back door was open to let fresh air in to the kitchen.

He walked in and headed straight to the office. He saw the man in the cheap suite sitting behind a desk. Their eyes made contact as Jack walked right in. The man behind the desk stood up. "Who the fuck are you?" he said with a stern yet quivering voice. Jack without reply grinned. His eyes glistened with a yellow tint. His fangs protruded from his gums, and he gently closed the door behind him.

2

The year is 1334. The woods were damp, and thick. Yet they were as inviting as the sun was bright and soothing. A robin was perched on a tree branch picking at the bark. The robin lifted his head and stretched its feathers out as far as they can go. Just as it began to groom itself it heard the crack of a tree branch below. Startled, the bird took off in flight. As the robin soared thru the sky it glanced to see a castle in the distance, and in the foreground was a well-dressed young eight year old Jack running as fast as he could. He was jumping over logs, turning and twisting in and out of trees, and as he came to a quick stop he turned. He hid behind a tree overlooking a dirt path. He heard footsteps getting closer as he kept his back to the tree. Trying his best not to be seen. The footsteps he was hearing seemed to have gotten even closer and have slowed from a run to a walk.

The Blood of Royals

Confidently hidden, he crouched down into attack mode and as the footsteps couldn't get any closer he jumped out.

"Ah ha," he yelled as he leaped out from behind the tree.

A pair of tiny hands grabbed him by his shirt in midair and, in one fluid motion took him down to the ground and sat upon his chest. It was a young peasant girl named Sarah with dark brown hair and big green eyes. Her hands were holding on to his shirt collar as his hands were grasping tightly to her forearms. Just as the breath returned to his lungs from hitting the ground. "I got you." was heard from his breath as he exhaled.

"Me?" she said with a smile "looks to be the other way around to me." She grabbed his hand in hers, helping him to his feet. "Besides, girls are naturally way faster than boys."

"No there not!" he replied. "I can beat you anytime, anywhere."

"OK, first one to the well wins" she said as they both crouched down.

"Lord Jackson?" they heard in the distance.

Stopping in their tracks they both glanced behind to see how far back the voice was coming from. Judging that it was a good ways away. They turned their heads, looked each other in the eye and, said "Go!"

They took off down the road as fast as they could. They left nothing but dust to be seen as a man on horseback arrived. "Lord Jackson!?" the man yelled in exhaustion.

The man on horseback was Baldric an older gentleman visibly out of shape riding a horse that seems to be his equal. Baldric was Lord Jackson's tutor and caretaker. Noticeably tired he yelled out again "Lord Jackson!?" Out of breath he continued on his chase.

"You cheated!" Lord Jackson said as he reached the well.

"I surely did not!" Sarah replied as she started to pull up a bucket from the well. "I'm just faster than you."

Once she pulled the bucket out of the well she began to drink. She started to hand the bucket to Lord Jackson as Baldric arrived.

"Lord Jackson, Stop!" he yelled as he got off his horse. He pulled a leather canter from his person. "If your thirsty drink this. Young Lords do not drink from buckets." he said with disgust as he handed the canter to Lord Jackson.

Young Lord Jackson drank from the canter and tried to hand it off to Sarah so she too could have a drink. The old man grabbed it away, and placed it back upon his person.

"Sarah is my friend. She can have a drink if she wants one!" Lord Jackson demanded as he stomped his foot in anger.

"Lord Jackson, you know your father does not want you to be playing outside of the castle walls," Baldric stated as he grabbed him by the shoulder "Especially not with someone like her."

Lord Jackson kicked Baldric in the shin and yelled "I don't care what my father says!" Then he grabbed Sarah by the hand and they ran back into the woods to play.

For the next six years despite his father's wishes, Lord Jackson and Sarah stayed the closest of friends. This year however marked Lord Jackson's 14th year of life and his ascension into manhood. His father Prince Edward, known as 'The Black Prince' is to throw his son a grand ball in honor of his big day. Word has been sent to every noble Lord and Lady in the kingdom that on the 21st day of April in the year 1340, there is to be the biggest and most amazing masquerade ball to ever be witnessed by man.

Lord Jackson, tired of his studies, sat at a desk with an old book in front of him. Unable to focus, Lord Jackson couldn't keep from looking out the window to see Sarah playing in a nearby field. Wishing he was outside with her he began to daydream that he was out there with her running and jumping, laughing and...

SMACK! A switch was slapped against the desk to get his attention. Baldric stepped between Lord Jackson and the window holding the switch in his hand.

"You know your party is in two days, and I thought you said you wanted to make your father proud."

"Of course I do" Lord Jackson replied.

"Then you need to concentrate."

"I know this all backwards and forwards." Lord Jackson proclaimed. "I'm drained. I just need a break."

Baldric looked deep into Lord Jackson's eyes and saw the desperation. He bent over getting face to face, nose to nose and tells Lord Jackson "OK, go."

"Really?"

"Yes Really. You have been working very hard. So I concede. Go play."

Lord Jackson jumped from his chair and ran out the door.

Baldric yelled out to Lord Jackson as he left. "Make sure you are washed and properly dressed for dinner. You wouldn't want to upset your father."

Lord Jackson ran out to the field where he last saw his friend Sarah. As he arrived he looked all over and she was nowhere to be seen. He called out her name.

"Sarah!"

He headed to a path in the woods just

beyond the field that they have played in millions of times before. He entered the path yelling out her name again. Before he could yell her name a third time he felt a hand reach from behind him and cover his mouth.

"Shh." Sarah whispered. "Quickly, follow me." she said as she ran and jumped for cover behind a pile of logs.

"What is it?" he whispered as he followed behind her.

"Trolls." she answered. "The kingdom is being attacked by trolls and, it's up to us to save it." She reached her hand out to Lord Jackson. "Together?"

Lord Jackson grabbed her wrist as she grabbed his. "Forever!" he replied. They both went forth grabbing the biggest sticks they could find. They leapt out onto the field and started to battle the trolls.

With the last of the trolls finally defeated. They both fell back into the deep grass of the field to relax. They both laid there motionless with the warmth of the sun hitting their faces as they simultaneously burst into laughter.

"So my party is in two days." Lord Jackson brought up. "My father says it is only for royalty. I told him I wanted you to be there but, he said no."

Disappointed Sarah replied "That's OK. I can see you after."

"I don't know. I might not be able to see you after the party. I actually might not be able to see you for some time afterward."

Lord Jackson sat up to explain further. "I

have to go thru something called a Tegmine Somnum and I don't know how long it will take. I'm told it's different for everyone who goes thru it."

Sarah stayed laid out on the ground. Lord Jackson saw the disappointment in her eyes.

"Though, I think I might know how you can sneak in to the party. Everyone is going to be in masks. If I can, I will get you a mask and dress. I will leave it at the opening at the east wall."

"Are you sure?"

"Yes, you're my best friend and I want you to be there. It wouldn't be a party without you. Once you change into the dress and mask you will be able to just slip right in with the other guests. No one will ever know."

"OK, I am in." she said with a smile.

"Oh no." Lord Jackson said as he realized the time. He Jumped to his feet. "I have to go."

"That's OK. I have to go too. Will I see you tomorrow?"

"Of course, I heard there's a dragon that has been eating the livestock. It's up to us to hunt it down and save the kingdom."

They both giggled and headed their separate ways. The sun began to set and Lord Jackson ran home as fast as his feat could go.

On the morning of his party Lord Jackson was feeling very nervous. He had a very strange feeling in the pit of his stomach and was not sure why. As he eased out of bed he looked around the room and noticed sitting in the corner of his windowsill was a large red apple. This was something he had seen many times before and it was something that made him smile more and more every time he did. This was a secret signal he and Sarah had worked out to say good morning on special occasions.

As he rose and walked toward the window he realized there was a note tucked under the apple. He sat in the window sill with the apple in one hand and the note in the other. He took a big bite out of the apple as he read the note that simply said "Good morning, May this day of your birth grant you much happiness. With a warm heart and well wishes I will be counting the moments till I see you tonight."

With a smile he took one last bite from the apple. He walked over to a highly polished white steel mirror hanging on the wall. He looked himself in the eye, puffed up his chest, and thought to himself 'So this is what a man looks like'. Next to it hung a white mask fit for a masquerade of epic proportions. It was made of the finest leather and the most precious of stones. There had never been a finer mask ever made. He placed the apple on the armoire and grabbed the mask wrapping the ribbon around his head. Looking into the mirror he gave himself a smile.

Seamlessly time elapsed forward to the evening of the masquerade ball. Lord Jackson took one last glance at himself in a mirror located in the hall just before he made his grand entrance in to the ball.

The entrance to the ball was opened by two servants in masks. Lord Jackson entered the room and as he walked out to the balcony at the top of the stairs he looked out in amazement to a crowd of people in masks who were there just for him. He scanned the crowd for Sarah, and after a few seconds he saw her in the back. She smiled. He smiled, and as he started to walk to her, his father walked up beside him grabbing him by the shoulder to address the crowd.

"My Lords and Ladies, I welcome you here tonight to celebrate Lord Jackson and the beginning of his journey into man hood." Prince Edward said as he looked at his son grinning with admiration, squeezing his son closer. He continued as he looked back to the crowd "I have waited 14 long years for this night and it makes me proud for he is finally joining the ranks of our highest and our mightiest."

Sarah looked on with such joy and curiosity for even though she had been friends with Lord Jackson most of their childhood she had never attend any of the functions in the castle until that night. If it weren't for Lord Jackson advising her of how to sneak in and out she may not have ever seen such grandeur. As she started her way thru the crowd to get to her friend a bell rang and the Prince announced the evening's meal was now ready and the crowd shifted to make their way to the dining hall.

The dining hall was just to the west of the ball room and was rich in an abundance of the finest of food and drink.

On their way to the ballroom Prince Edward pulled Lord Jackson aside "Baldrick assured me that you have been working hard and you are quite ready for tonight. Tonight you are not just another year older but you are embarking on a new beginning"

Lord Jackson nodded his head and said "Yes Father."

"Good, then you are aware your body is going to be going thru certain changes now. Changes that will make you superior both physically and mentally above any mere mortal. And with these changes comes a responsibility, not only to our people who depend on us but also to our Family. Everyone here is your family Jackson. Do you understand?"

"I do." Lord Jackson replied.

"Are you hungry?"

"I am."

"Good, let us eat." the prince said as he lead his son to the dining hall.

Lord Jackson saw Sarah and grabbed her hand as they sat for the meal. When they sat down at the table, servants came by with towels, ewers of water, and a basins. They washed their hands in a stream of water poured by the servants and dried them with the towels just before they ate.

During the meal they were entertained by jugglers and minstrels. Lord Jackson was as happy as he had ever been. Loving glances were shared between him and Sarah. Along with his father's professions of pride this was turning out to be the greatest day of his life.

After the meal they all headed back to the ballroom. A band of minstrels were playing and the crowd was filled with people dancing and having a great time. The music was a loft as Lord Jackson grabbed Sarah by the hand and dragged her to the dance floor.

The night was filled with dance and love was in the air. The time flew as the masquerade went on and on.

The time reached midnight and chimes began to ring. Prince Edward stopped the music and once again began to address the crowd.

"Lord Jackson, my son, please come to my side."

With a bow Lord Jackson raised Sarah's hand to his lips and kissed it while he looked deep into her eyes. He gave her a smile and turned to join his father at the back of the room.

He reached his father's side. The chimes that were getting progressively louder finally come to a silence.

"This, my son, is your time." Prince Edward started to proclaim as a young woman was heard screaming in the background.

"This is your time to grow into manhood. Your time to take your place in this world, and your time to taste your royal birth right. A birthright passed on for many generations thru the blood of our ancestors. This my son, is your immortality." his father said with a smile as two big wooden doors opened.

A part in the crowd slowly formed as men in hooded gowns carried in a young woman bound to a wooden table. The woman was a red headed girl with bright green eyes without a stitch of clothing to her body. Her scream at this point had turned to a whimper of disbelief. Which quickly turned to an exhausted inability to scream due to the sore and over worked muscles in her throat.

The crowd looked on with excitement as the girl was laid at Lord Jackson's feet. Hunger was in the eyes of the crowd, yet Sarah looked on with caution and great fear. She tried her hardest not to let on to how frightened she truly was. As the crowd closed in on Lord Jackson, Sarah eased her way to an exit scared as to what she was about to witness.

Lord Jackson began to focus on what he had been taught. His years of training had been leading him to this very moment. As he bowed his head, he drank from the goblet that was handed to him by his father, the crowd became silent, and he began to read aloud from a large book that was held in front of him by two hooded servants.

"A caelo usque ad centrum, a capite ad calcem, beati possidentes, concilio et labore, concordia cum veritate, carpe cruor regia."

Lord Jackson lifted his head with his eyes aglow. He let out a scream, not from his lungs but through his eyes for the light had become so sensitive even the air around his corneas caused an intense pain. He opened his mouth and fangs pierced through his gums making his teeth ache and bleed. His head felt like it was going to explode at any moment. He felt his heart pound stronger than he had ever felt before. With an unimaginable force of pure hunger pushing him forward, the pain in his head reached a numbing point and as he ascended upon the girl's body and took his first bite. His fangs pierced her skin and his mouth was immediately filled with her warm blood and as he ingested, her blood coursed through his body with a cool chill that eased every ache he had. It even relieved ones he didn't even know he had.

After a few pints were drained from her body he raised his head gasping for air with such pure relief. Feeling truly quenched and truly whole for the first time since he was born.

Sarah, with a single tear running down her cheek, calmly and quietly eased her way thru the back door.

The moons reflection was seen thru the still water that filled an open barrel. The barrel stood all alone at the end of a long poorly lit dock. A slight ripple started flowing thru the water causing the reflection of the moon to break up into tiny little specks of light. The ripples got rougher as feet were felt running down the dock.

"God help us all..." is yelled by a man as he crashed into the barrel causing the barrel to burst open and water to spill out onto the dock and into the river. The man who was now soaking wet and on the ground amidst the ruble seemed to have been attacked. His face, bloodied and bruised, had been scratched as if done by some kind of wild animal. The blood ran down his face to his shoulder then down the back of his arm and into the water causing it to soil and slowly turn red.

The Blood of Royals

The man wiped his eyes and looked down the dock. A straggling figure emerged above the man with his hands outreached. A lamp was lit above. It was flickering directly behind the figure, and the man could not see who had so kindly come to help him in his time of need.

"Please help me..." he said in exhaustion as he reached his hand out to the stranger.

He quickly made the unfortunate connection that the figure he saw before him was not actually there to help. It was one of the undead who have been terrorizing the town. It was a creature whom death had clearly taken its soul, but left nothing but hunger in its eyes. When his arm was grabbed it was placed very forcefully into the creature's mouth. Teeth were sunk into the man's flesh, and with the pain from his flesh being ripped from his body the man let out a blood curdling scream.

The scream was undeniably heard by a young boy who was hiding about four hundred meters away on the other end of the dock against a storage building within a stack of barrels. The scream caused the boy to scurry farther back within the barrels, hitting his head on the barrel above. This in return caused some of the water to spill from the barrel covering the boy. He was now wet from head to toe. Soaked and shivering in fear.

The boy heard a constant screaming for help coming from all directions in many different voices. He sat curled up in the darkness and began to hear someone or something crawl towards the barrels. He heard a slow gnarly groaning and grunting getting closer and closer as he sat frozen in fear.

The boy was able to see thru a small space between the barrels and saw that the creature he was hearing was getting closer to him. It looked almost human but seemed to be missing most of the flesh from its face, hands, and body. He also noticed it was missing its legs and as it was coming closer it was dragging its body by its forearms causing the flesh from the arms and body to become loose and peel away with every push forward.

The creature was now close enough to the barrels that it could smell the young boy's fresh flesh and was now trying to reach him thru the barrels. The boy was franticly trying to kick the hand away, and was now screaming for help himself.

The sound of a horse drew near and the boy, thru the crack of the barrel, saw the horse's huff smash thru the top of the creatures head. The boy saw the hand that was once intent on trying to grab him had now dropped to a limp lifeless calm.

Through the top of the barrels the boy saw a black glove reaching down open handed towards him. The boy looked past the glove and saw a young man on a horse. The man yelled out to him "Grab my hand, I will bring you to safety!" The boy reached his hand out and was pulled out and away from the barrels and onto the horse.

The man on the horse was Lord Jackson now 4 years older. He told the boy to hold on tight, and as he rode off he pulled out his sword. He started stabbing and lobbing off the heads of each creature he rode by. The boy clung to his back and buried his head trying to avoid the sights of the mayhem around him.

As they rode away from the town towards the castle the creatures began to become fewer and farther apart. They rode by an old barn and the boy who had kept his eyes shut tight for a good ten minutes prior heard a scream come from a familiar woman's voice.

As he poked his eye open in curiosity he saw a young teenage girl with blonde curls being torn apart and eaten by a larger older man. She had on a blue dress that was hanging halfway off her body. The man had her pined to the ground about ten feet from the barn. Yet all the boy could focus on was her face screaming in agony. Her eyes seemed to stare straight into his soul.

As the boy closed his eyes once again to hide away from the world around him, a tear fell down his cheek. He grabbed on to Lord Jackson tighter than before. Lord Jackson placed his hand over the boy's tightly clutched fists and just held his hand there in an attempt to comfort him.

6

Moments earlier a teenage boy peeked his head thru two giant barn doors. He slowly looked around very cautiously. He walked slowly over to a stack of hay trying his hardest not to make a sound. He reached the side of the hay stack, and jumped out in an attempt to scare the young woman who he had expected was going to be there.

Disappointed that she was not there he sat at the bottom of the stack. After a couple of minutes he saw a few pieces of straw land on his lap and as he started to wonder where they came from, he heard a rustling from above. As he turned to look above he was tackled to the ground by a beautiful young girl in a blue dress and blonde curls.

"Oh I got you this time." she proclaimed. They both start to laugh and he quickly rolled and turned her over so he was now on top of her.

"Who's got who?" he asked as he began to tickle her.

"OK, OK, stop you win!" she attempted to say in the midst of her laughter.

He eased up and let her go. As they both sat up and looked into each other's eyes deeply and intently, they began to kiss. He laid her down on the hay stack and just as he started to unlace her dress, he stopped.

"What about your father? What if he catches us?" he asked as his finger brushed over her nipple as it was poking thru the fabric of her dress.

"Don't worry about him. He has been sick all day and hasn't even been able to get out of bed."

"Is he OK?" he asked.

"Do you really want to talk about my father right now?" she said as she started to pull down the top of her dress revealing her breasts.

He leaned into her neck and began to kiss just below her ear. The smell from her hair was sweet and he playfully nibbled at her earlobe. His hand found its way to her soft smooth breast and began to caress his way to her nipple. The palm of his hand lifted the bottom of her breast just slightly. Just enough to squeeze and slowly message her nipple ever so lightly between his fingers.

He continued to kiss his way down to the spot just above her collarbone. Her nipples were completely erect. He started to kiss lower and lower until his lips wrapped around her nipple sucking it ever so lightly tickling the tip of the nipple with his tongue.

Just as his mouth had reached her breast her hand had wondered its way to his leg. She began to caress his leg starting from his knee to his inner thigh. She squeezed his leg each time she moaned with pleasure.

His hand smoothly made its way down her rib cage to her hip continuing over her dress to her knee. Taking each moan from her mouth as an invitation to go further his hand started to travel back from where it came going farther and farther up her thigh. This time keeping his hand pressed to her smooth skin raising her dress with every inch forward.

They both heard a loud groan come from the front of the barn and realizing that it was not their own. They came to an immediate halt. They both looked out of the corner of their eyes and saw her father standing in the opening of the barn doors. She jumped to cover herself as best she could. “Papa? This isn't what it looks like!” she started to explain as her father’s grunt got louder. The father started walking towards them.

“Sir, I know you are worried about your daughter!” the boy started to say as he walked toward her father. “But I want you to know. I am in love with her and I would never do anything to bring shame to her or your family.”

The father walked closer and let out another grunt. The boy took this as a sign of acceptance and got on his knees just in front of the father.

“Sir, I would be honored if I could have your daughters hand in....” he started to say, and just before he could get the rest of the words from his mouth the father grabbed the boy's head and bites the flesh from his forehead. The father forced the boy down to the ground and proceeded to eat at his face. The girl could not believe what she is seeing and was paralyzed by the boys screams. She was left breathless from bearing witness to the pure horror right in front of her eyes. The very moment she was able to catch her breath she let out such a blood curdling scream that her father turned from the boy and focused his hunger toward her.

She jumped up and started to run. She knew she had to make it past her father who was between her and the only way out. She leapt over the boy's body just barely squeaking by her father who grabbed her leg in mid jump, causing her to hit the ground. She rolled out of reach and as she got up to run she realized there was skin missing from her shin. She looked back to see her father had the skin in his hand. He stood up and started to walk toward her. He placed the skin in his mouth and began to chew.

She hobbled out of the barn unable to run, and only got about ten feet from the barn when she felt his hands on her shoulders forcing her to the ground. She landed face down on the ground. Before she could lift herself up she felt his teeth piercing thru the skin on her back tearing the tendons straight from her spine. The pain was so intense her eyes began to water. Through her blurred vision she caught a glimpse of a man on horseback. She reached her hand out in an attempt to plead for help. She tried to scream but the pain was so intense that the only thing leaving her lungs was silence.

7

A big wooden door swung open to a hidden laboratory deep within the bowels of the castle. Prince Edward walked in and walked straight to an elderly man in a black hooded cloak. The man was thin, hunched over, and had a long salt and pepper beard that stretched down to his waist with a frail head of hair to match. The man was in deep thought and was writing in a book.

"Is it ready for the final push?" Prince Edward inquired. "There is a war brewing right under our feet. I need this finished now!"

"Sire, the results are strong, but there are still so many tests I need to run..."

Prince Edward slammed the book on the man's hand looked him dead in the eyes and threatened "I want this to be finished and deployed by the end of this week. And if it is not done I will have your head. Do you understand me?"

"Yes Sire." the man stated as his hand was set free. He clutched his hand to his chest and continued "as you wish. Your will be done."

Prince Edward walked past a row of cages that were filled with people and stopped to look at one of the captives. "It better be. Now, I have a masquerade to get ready for." He pointed to a red headed girl in the cage. "Have this one prepped and prepared for tonight. She will be perfect. My son deserves the best on his big day."

As he left through the door he reiterated "The end of the week!" And the door slammed behind him.

The cloaked man grabbed his cane and walked to the cage so he can begin to prepare the girl with red hair for tonight. He grabbed a cup from a nearby table and held it in front of her cage. She quickly crawled to the front of the cage reaching out for the cup. He held it just out of her reach until she calmed down then handed it to her to drink. She was so dehydrated she grabbed the cup and drank without hesitation.

The man in the next cage reached thru the bars and begged. "Please kind sir, give me some water as I am not feeling well. Please sir." The cloaked man rapped the man's hands with his cane. And the man backed up into the corner of his cage.

The girl with red hair started to get light headed and passed out. The cloaked man opened the big wooden door and had the guards that were in the corridor come in to retrieve the girl from the cage. The cloaked man pointed to a big wooden board covered in straps. The two men removed the girl from the cage and removed what little bit of clothing was attached to her body. They strapped her down and the cloaked man began to sponge her down and clean her up. As the man in the cage looked on to what was happening he cowered in the corner and began to cough profusely.

8

The sun set thru the trees as an orange glow whispered thru the leaves. A mist flowed along the grass with a red tint that grew darker and darker with each second to pass. Just as the moon rose, after his body had been asleep for days, so did Lord Jackson's eyes. With a long stretch and a crack of his neck he felt refreshed and ready to take on the world. Unsure how long he had been out, memories of the ball play in his head of him and Sarah creating a smile on his face. He rose out of bed to a haunting yet familiar smell he just couldn't place.

He turned to the windowsill to see if Sarah had left an apple for him. To his dismay it was not. In its place he saw a goblet that seemed to beckon him like a moth to a flame. He opened the curtains to bask in the moonlight as he drank.

He looked out upon his kingdom. He got an unsettling feeling in the pit of his heart yet as he stared out the window he saw nothing to condone his uneasiness. Though he just couldn't seem to shake the feeling that something is just not right.

Lord Jackson got dressed for the day and headed to see his father. He found his father in his study hovering over a table that contained a large-scale map of his land and its surrounding kingdoms.

"I see you're finally awake. Did you drink? I had a goblet left for you for when you woke." Prince Edward asked "There is more there if you want more." He said as he pointed to a pitcher and some goblets near the door. "HA! That's it" he proclaimed as he moved a few red blocks strategically about the table.

"How long have I been asleep father?" Inquired Lord Jackson.

"Five days!" the Prince replied.

Lord Jackson was surprised it had been that long and started to think of how worried Sarah might be.

Without Lord Jackson being able to get another word from his mouth, his father continued. "I envy you my son. This first year is going to be such a remarkable time for you. Your body will teach you things that you never would have thought to be possible. Your senses are all heightened to a point that you swear god himself is talking and walking directly thru you."

Prince Edward poured two goblets and handed one to his son. "That is why I want you to stay here and be my eyes and ears when I go to Spain tomorrow."

"Oh Father, Please may I go with you? You said yourself I am a man now."

"Not this time my son. I need you here. I need you to be the head of this house while I'm away."

"But Father Please?"

"I said no, and that's it." The prince said sternly.

Lord Jackson stood there disappointed.

The prince threw his arm over Lord Jackson's shoulders. "Come my son, soon you will get your chance and one day we will conquer this land together. For some day it will all be ours."

Lord Jackson awoke after a 12 hour slumber, recuperating after the 18th birthday party his friends thru him the night before. He had now grown into the man he was meant to be. Now refreshed and energized there was only one person he wanted to see.

Sarah asleep in her bed, was woken up by the sound of rocks hitting her floor. With a squint of her eyes she heard her name being whispered from afar. She eased her way to the open windowsill. A smile rushed over her face.

"You shouldn't be here." she yelled out the window with a whisper just loud enough to be heard.

"I need to see you, I miss you." Lord Jackson said as he stood next to his horse. "Please, come down."

"Meet me at the well in ten minutes" she

said as she faded back from the windowsill.

Lord Jackson, once there tied his horse to a tree near the well and waited. He sat on the edge of the well, and pulled a handkerchief from his pocket. As he opened the kerchief he removed a small circular gold brooch that was covered in jewels. Lord Jackson breathed heavily upon it and proceeded to clean it off. He held it up to the sun to see it shine. He wrapped it back up and placed it back into his pocket.

Sarah arrived a few minutes later. Lord Jackson went to give her a hug and she backed off.

"You've missed me?" she asked.

"I did." he replied as he stepped closer.

"Just how much have you missed me?"

"I've missed you more than a leper misses his ..."

"OK, OK," she said with a chuckle and a smile. "Thank you, I needed a good laugh."

"What's wrong?" he asked as he wrapped his arms around her waist.

"I am just exhausted. My parents have both been sick since yesterday. I have been working myself ragged trying to do as much as I can so they don't have to."

"What can I do to help?"

"I don't know. Just hold me for a moment."

They both sat on the ground perched in each other's arms while resting their backs on the well. Lord Jackson ran his fingers thru her hair as she laid her head upon his chest.

"I have something for you that might make you feel a little bit better." He brought up as he reached into his pocket.

She sat up a bit and asked "Really?"

"Take a look." he told her as he handed her the handkerchief.

She opened it up and she began to tear up. "It's beautiful."

"It was my mothers. And I want you to have it."

"I can't accept this."

"Yes, you can." he said as he wrapped her hands around it.

"Thank you. I love you so much." She wrapped her arms around his neck and gave him a kiss. She rested her head back on his chest and started to weep.

"What's wrong?" he asked as he caressed the back of her head.

"I'm just worried that's all. I know you told me we should take it one day at a time, but I just can't help but think of how this won't end well. I love you. I do, but what's going to happen when we get older?"

"We can't think of that right now."

"We have to. Your father is going to want you to produce an heir soon, and we both know we can't marry unless I'm part of the same blood line."

"I can't... No, I won't change you. You weren't born into it. You don't know what you're asking."

She looked him deep in his eyes, "I know I want to be with you. I know I want a life with you. And I know that's not possible if you don't."

"It is possible. And trust me you wouldn't want me to change you even if I could. For one it's a pain like you have never felt before. Since you were not born into it it's not even guaranteed you would make it thru. And I can't lose you like that." he took her by the hands. "I won't lose you like that."

Feeling his sincerity and slight desperation to move on from this subject she decided not to push it any further. "OK, we can make this work without." She attached the brooch to her dress and looked him in the eyes. "I love it."

"Let's go to the lake. We can spend the whole day there." he suggested.

"I can't." she replied. "My parents, there ill and there so much I need to take care of."

"That's right, I forgot."

Lord Jackson got up and walked over to his horse. He looked to Sarah. "Let's go," he told her. "Get on. I am not leaving your side today. My hands are yours. Just tell me how I can help."

"You're going to help me with the house work?" she chuckled with a smile. "OK, let's see if we can get those hands dirty."

Sarah threw her leg over and onto the horse. Lord Jackson grabbed the reigns looked the horse in the eyes and let out a 'humph'.

They arrive to Sarah's home. The air was calm and an eerie chill ran across both of their skins.

The Blood of Royals

The moon was bright and full. They looked into each other's eyes as Lord Jackson tied up his horse. Sarah eased off the steed and no sooner then as her feet touched ground they hear a loud crashing sound come from inside the house.

They rushed inside to see furniture thrown about. Two figures were crouched down in the shadowed corner. The noise of entering the room was heard by the two figures as they stood there and turned towards Lord Jackson and Sarah. Both figures bore a strong resemblance to Sarah's parents but something was not quite right. For a split second there was a calmness in the air but that quickly turned to nerves as they heard nothing but heavy grunting and breathing coming from the shadowy figures before them.

With a struggle to speak, nervously Sarah called out "Mom? Dad?"

Lord Jackson grabbed Sarah's hand to stop her from going any further into the room than what she had already. His other hand instinctively grabbed the handle of his sword in anticipation of what he felt was not going to be the welcoming they were expecting.

The two figures simultaneously started to sniff the air and their eyes became wider. They started walking toward Lord Jackson and Sarah getting faster and faster.

Lord Jackson drew his sword and Sarah started to yell. "What are you doing? Those are my parents. There just sick. Put that away and help me get them back into bed."

Sarah broke her hand away and walked

to

her parents. She put one hand on her mother's shoulder while she grabbed her mother's hand with the other.

In the same momentum her parents still urged forward. They both opened there mouths as wide as inhumanly possible and let out a scream that could only be described as empty yet filled with a tone of hunger as if they had not eaten anything in over a thousand years. It was disturbingly haunting and immediately put Lord Jackson and Sarah on their toes.

At that moment Sarah's mother attempted to take a bite out of Sarah's arm. With quick and nimble reflexes Sarah was able to avoid her mother's teeth sinking deep into her flesh. She was able to push her mother back, but her father began to attack Lord Jackson.

Lord Jackson placed his foot to her father's chest and kicked him away. The father went flying thru the air, and Lord Jackson was able to draw his sword and place it to her mother's throat. Not as an attempt to fatally wound her but more like an attempt to stop her in her tracks.

Even with his sword to her throat Sarah's mother still pushed forward. With no visible acknowledgment to the pain she pushed her own body forward causing the sharp blade of the sword to start cutting thru her own flesh. Her mouth, in a chomping motion, was still attempting to bite at her own daughter. The more she chomped forward the deeper the sword seemed to bury itself into her neck.

Lord Jackson, not wanting to decapitate Sarah's mother unintentional or otherwise in front of her, removed his sword from her throat and grabbed her by her shoulders. He forced her down to the ground next to the father.

Sarah saw pieces of broken furniture protruding thru her father's chest and mother's leg. It was keeping them both pinned to the ground. Their mouths kept chomping away biting at the air as if they could somehow reach them from where they were. It all happened so fast, and in that moment Sarah was able to catch her breath and truly look at her parents. She took a moment to take it all in and let out a blood curdling scream.

Lord Jackson grabbed her and pulled her head to his chest. Letting it all out she could now see that her parents where nothing but a shell of who they were. Tears flew down her face as she tried to comprehend why this had just happened. Lord Jackson kept her wrapped in his arms as they both stood there in shock.

"What is wrong with them? What is going on?" she started to question. "They were just fine two days ago. Just last night they were complaining of headaches and a fever. This morning they said they felt stiffness in their legs and arms and they were both nauseous. I was out most of the day picking some wormwood, mint, and lemon balm for them. And now look at them. They look like the angel of death has come to take them away but then decided to leave them behind." She turned and put her face into Lord Jackson's chest. They turn to leave, and Sarah pauses "We can't leave them like this."

Lord Jackson eased Sarah outside. “I will take care of this.” he held her face as he wiped her tears. “You don't need to see any more.”

He turned to go back in and closed the door behind him. Sarah’s legs could no longer hold her up as she fell to her knees. She buried her face in the morning dew of the grass and began to cry.

10

There was an urgency in the air as a young peasant boy was pulling a bucket of water from the nearby well. Pulling with all his might he was trying to get as much water out of the well as he could. The bucket made its way to the top and was filled to the brim. The boy's arms were shaking and feeling weak for this was already his third trip. He connected two buckets to a long pole one on each end and carried it on the back of his neck and shoulders. He tried his best to balance and not spill a drop. His mother was home sick and he was in a hurry to bring it to her.

Even though his arms were week, his will was strong. With the buckets weighing him down his legs were moving his little body as fast and as careful as they could. By the time he had reached his mother's bedside his frail little body had almost given out.

The Blood of Royals

Seeing his mother in such a state. Rest was the furthest thing from his mind. He grabbed a ladle and dipped it into the bucket filling it with water. Water dripped from the ladle with every step as he brought it to his mother. Slowly raising it to her mouth he took notice as to how he was spilling little by little all over his mother. He tried to make more of a conscious effort not to spill anther drop.

As the ladle got to his mother's mouth she forcefully grabbed her sons hand and bit down with all her might. Her teeth ripped through her son's skin as he dropped the ladle. He spilled the water all over his mother and the bed she laid upon. The ladle hit the floor making a clinking sound. It triggered a shock to the son's brain causing him to focus solely on the pain that was throbbing from his hand. He lets out a scream and pulled his hand away from his mother's mouth.

With his hand clinched to his chest he ran out of the house screaming in pain. He yelled out at the top of his lungs "Father!" Tears were flowing from his face as he ran through the field to get to his father's workshop. His father was the town blacksmith. He had been hard at work all morning and he will surely know what to do. The boy ran with every inch of energy he had left. Stumbling and picking himself up, he finally made it.

His father was covered in sweet, and ceased all that he was doing as soon as his son burst thru the door. Dripping in blood and coughing profusely his son tried his hardest to explain to his father what had just happened. Before he could utter a word he collapsed from exhaustion right into his father's arms. His father trying to piece together what had just happened held his son tight and started to run his fingers through his son's hair.

He took a closer look at his son and noticed blood all over his clothes and started to examine him to see where it was coming from. As he started, his son began convulsing and coughing up blood. His father quickly picked up his boy in one arm and with the other arm he cleared away the debris from the nearest table. He laid his son down and the convulsing stopped, but so did his breathing.

In a panic his father yelled out for help. Dropping to his knees he started to pray. "Dear heavenly father please don't let my son die please help him. Please send someone who can help. He has never harmed a soul. He is a good boy. Please don't take him from me yet."

He jumped up from his knees and ran outside to find help. Yelling at the top of his lungs his cries for help were heard by a nun picking herbs nearby. Hearing the pure desperation in the cry for help she dropped what she was doing and ran to assist.

The blacksmith saw her, and as she got close he grabbed her by the arm and brought her into his workshop. He tried to explain what had just happened as best he could.

"How long has he been like this?" she asked.

"I don't know, it all happened just now. He ran in the door screaming and then collapsed."

The Blood of Royals

She placed her head to the boy's chest. She tried to listen for a heartbeat but she was not able to hear one. With sadness she closed her eyes. It brought an ache to her heart knowing she had to now let this blacksmith know his son was gone. As she tried to speak she felt a lump in her throat preventing her from forming the words. So she simply grabbed a nearby blanket and started to cover him up.

Seeing the sadness in her eyes as she laid the blanket over his body the father new right then that he would never hear his boy's contagious laugh again. He would never again hear his son whistle or call for his father's help. The tears started to flow from his eyes uncontrollably as he plopped down onto a stool.

As the nun placed the blanket over the boy her hands got close to his face. The boy's eyes shot open wide, and in an instant he then grabbed the nun's arm forcefully shoving it into his mouth and began to chew.

The father, whose face was buried in his hands, heard the nun let out a scream. He jumped up from the stool he was sitting on and bumped into his cooling station which was filled with swords, daggers and shields.

The son grabbed tightly to the nuns clothes and as the nun tried to pull away. She jumped back causing momentum that helped the son lung forward allowing him to begin eating at the nuns face and neck.

Frightened by the actions he was witnessing the father grabbed one of the many swords from the table. The clattering of the swords got the attention of the little boy. The father saw the hunger in the boy's eyes and feared it was a possession from Satan himself. He pointed the sword at his son.

His son charged toward him with an unnatural speed. The blacksmith nervously aimed the sword directly at his boy's chest and as he got closer the boy ran straight into the sharp blade piercing himself deeper with every foot forward.

Continuing his attack, the boy kept chomping and biting at the air trying to reach his father's flesh. The boy kept pushing forward sliding closer and closer up the blade. The father with his free hand grabbed a second sword and swung it at his boy's neck, and in one swift motion lobed off the head of his only son.

11

A butcher's knife slammed thru a chicken's freshly broken and plucked neck as it made contact with the butchers block beneath it. The chickens head rolled to the floor and landed next to the cook's feet. The cook was a tall thick hairy man with less teeth than any of the animals he had killed. He tied the chicken's feet and hung it up to drain its blood.

The alewife burst into the room with dishes in her hands, and as she threw them into a bucket filled with water she glanced out the window to see the sun setting and sighed in exhaustion. She grabbed two clean wooden bowls and filed them with stew that had been cooking all day in a large black kettle. She took a deep breath, kicked open the door, and entered the main room. She dropped the bowls off at a table on her way back to behind the bar.

"Thanks Emma." the old patron about to stuff his mouth full of stew said before he took his first bite.

"Anytime Gabriel. Your Ale is on its way sweetie." she replied as she started to poor the ale from a barrel stacked behind the bar.

Emma was a young woman whose parents passed away a few years prior. She, unlike most the other people in her village was an only child and to make ends meet she began making and serving ale as her own mother did before her.

The ale her mother made was the talk of the land and people would come from far and wide for just a taste. Since her parents death she had made quite a few upgrades which took the family business to a whole other level.

As she gave Gabriel his ale, the door to the tavern swung open. Lord Jackson, Sarah, the Blacksmith, and two knights burst in. Lord Jackson and the men started to barricade the doors and windows. Sarah ran over to Emma.

Emma Started yelling "What are you doing?"

With no response the men continued to barricade the windows and doors. Sarah grabbed Emma by the arm leading her toward the back of the room to tell her what was about to go down before she really lost her mind.

"Emma, listen to me right know. We are under attack. This is the safest place to be right now and we need to make sure all entrances and exits are blocked and secure."

The cook came from the back to see what the commotion was.

"Attacked? Attacked by who?" Emma yelled.

Sarah grabbed both Emma and the cook and drags them both to the back. "Listen to me! We do not have time for details right now. Right now we need to make sure the back here is secure." She looked at Emma. "Do you have more tables?"

A few days prior Lord Jackson and Sarah both on horseback rode straight thru the night ending at the castle door. Lord Jackson shouted for the castle door to be raised. Once inside the castle walls Lord Jackson dismounts his steed. He then ordered the guard to lower the gate, and to make sure he did not open it for anyone until he returned.

Sarah handed off both horses to the stable boy.

"Make sure they are washed and feed right away we may need them again soon"

"Yes milady" the boy said as he walked them to the stables.

Lord Jackson on his way into the castle with Sarah ran into his friend Edwin in the courtyard. Edwin and his twin brother Godwin were two of the most feared and respected knights in the kingdom. There swordsmanship was unparalleled by any other.

Lord Jackson grabbed Edwin close. “I need you to get your brother and meet me inside. I need your help. Something big is going down, and I need you both.”

“For you Jackson? Anything.” Edwin shouted out as Lord Jackson and Sarah went inside.

Edwin headed to the armory to locate Godwin. As he entered the armory he heard loud moaning and grunting noises coming from the back of the room.

“Godwin, are you back there?”

“Yeah, give me a moment I'm almost done.”

A ladies voice was heard “Godwin!?” followed closely by the sound of a SLAP!

“Alright, I'm done.” Godwin reluctantly replied.

A half-naked lady appeared from the back stopping in front of Edwin.

“Edwin.” she says with a wink and a curtsey before she continued out the door.

“Gwen.” he replied.

Godwin appeared from the back fastening his pants and stretching his jaw. “And what can I do for you kind brother of mine?”

They both walked out of the armory and head back into the castle.

“Jackson has requested our services. He said something big is going down.”

"It's about time. I was getting bored being confined to these walls like this."

"And do you really have to keep using my name like that?"

"Hey, I can't help it if they somehow think I'm you. Who am I to correct them and destroy their dreams?"

Edwin shook his head in dismay and they both chuckled. Edwin smacked his brother in the back of the head, put his arm around his shoulders and they proceeded to the castle.

13

Prince Edward was sitting on his throne when Lord Jackson and Sarah barged into the room. The room was filled with minstrels and dancers. Lord Jackson and Prince Edward locked eyes as they walked closer. The Prince could see the urgency in his son's eyes.

"Father, I need to speak to you. This is an emergency."

"Clear the room at once!" Prince Edward demanded as he rose to his feet signaling the guards to clear the room

The room cleared as Lord Jackson and Sarah were joined by Edwin and Godwin. The doors to the hall closed and Prince Edward sat back into his throne.

"OK. You have my undivided attention. What is so important?" he asked while he grabbed his goblet for a drink.

"Father, something is a wry with the peasants. They're getting sick by the droves and the sickness is spreading like wildfire. They seem to be attacking each other. The sick are spreading the sickness by attacking and biting the healthy." Lord Jackson explained. "We need to stop this before it gets out of control. Father, with your blessing I would like to put together a squad of my men and a few hundred soldiers to put a stop to this before it gets too late."

Prince Edward inquired "What is the cause of this sickness? Where did it come from?"

"I do not know father. It is like no other sickness I have ever known. They seem to be eating each other." Lord Jackson replied.

The twins looked each other in disbelief. Being they have never known Lord Jackson to be a teller of tall tales, they shook it off and stood strong beside their friend and leader.

"Eating each other?" questioned the Prince.

"Father I know how this sounds, but I speak the truth. Sarah's own parents were both stricken ill and after they attempted to take a bite out of there only daughters arm we had to put them down."

Prince Edward looked into Sarah's eyes. He immediately saw the pain she had buried within and attempted to console her. "I am truly sorry for your lose my child. If there is anything you need."

"Thank you my lord." Sarah replied. "But, What I need right now is to put an end to this before more people fall prey to this horrible sickness. It is spreading so fast that I fear if we do not get out there to stop this there will be no one left to protect."

"Father," Lord Jackson added "we could use as many soldiers as you can spare."

With a long face, Prince Edward reluctantly replied "Lord Jackson I have already sent our troops to Calais weeks ago. They are there as we speak awaiting my arrival. We were to leave in the morning to join them."

The group looked at each other in fear of what the prince will say next.

Prince Edward took a deep breath. "I will dispatch a rider and send back 500 soldiers to help in this quarantine. Until they arrive you will need to take the lead in this. I am placing my faith in all of you to handle this until they arrive." he said as he looked each and every one of them in the eyes.

Lord Jackson bowed as his friends follow suit "Thank you father we will not let you down. Once we have control of the situation we will join you in Calais for what will be a glorious victory."

A proud honor poured over the prince's heart as he looked his son in the eyes and nods in approval.

14

A crash was heard from the front window pane of the tavern and a hand started to squeeze its way thru two boards nailed across the window. The space between the boards was not quite enough space for the hand to actually fit. This caused the skin to start ripping and peeling away until the hand completely pushed thru. The hand pushed farther and farther in and the skin kept ripping up the forearm. The forearm was almost fully pushed thru when it was swiftly chopped off by a sword and fell to the floor. The sound of hands banging on the wood got louder and more intense.

Lord Jackson could see the fear and worries in the patron’s faces. Though there were only a few patrons in the tavern he felt he needed to comfort them somehow.

“Can I please have everyone's attention?

I would first like to assure to you all that there is nothing to fear as long as we stay in here and they stay out there." Lord Jackson Stated until he was so rudely interrupted.

"What's out there? What are those things?" one of the patrons blurt out with a fear in his throat.

Lord Jackson replied "We are not sure exactly, but what we do know is that there is some sort of plague infecting our friends and loved ones." he continued as he looked into the eyes of everyone in the room. "People are becoming ill and developing a hunger for human flesh. They are very aggressive and contagious. In mere moments from a single bite you too will become plagued. So whatever you do, do not allow yourself to get bitten."

The tavern wench Emma had been handing out ale to Lord Jackson's men as he spoke, and finally to Lord Jackson himself. Lord Jackson nodded and thanked Emma for the ale. He began to drink when he heard a slight cough from one of the patrons.
With concern he asked "Does anyone feel under the weather? Does anyone have a cold, a cough, chills, fever, anything?"

A slight cough was heard again from the same patron. Everyone turned to look at the man who was now growing concerned. In his own defense he quickly replied "I am not sick, I just choked a bit. I swear I am fine."

Godwin stepped closer to the man to get a better look. The man notices Godwin grasping the handle of his sword.

"I'm fine I swear." proclaimed the man one more time.

Emma whispered something into Lord Jackson's ear. Lord Jackson walked over to an elderly man in the corner and sat next to him. "Have no fear my friend. What is your name?"

"Gabriel, my lord." the old man's reply was followed by a stifled cough.

"How long have you been under the weather Gabriel?"

Starting to feel a bit scared the old man's hand started to shake a bit. Lord Jackson placed his hand over the old mans to calm him and ease his worries.

"Since yesterday my lord."

"Can you recall when you first started to feel sick?"

"It was right after I had my lunch my lord, I went out to do my chores, and as I was feeding my chickens I became ill."

"What did you have for lunch?"

"That morning I replenished my water supply from the well and since I had some leftovers from the fowl I had for dinner the night before I used it to make a stew."

"Did you come into contact with anyone that day?"

"No my lord. This has been the first time I have left my house in a while. My wife passed a year ago today and sick or not my lord, let's just say I needed some fresh air today."

"Understood my friend." Lord Jackson placed his hand on the old man's shoulder as he stood up. "Sorry for your loss."

Lord Jackson motioned for Emma to come over. "Can my friend here get another bowl of stew please?"

Emma smiled with acceptance. "Of course my lord, right away." She signaled for the cook to retrieve the stew from the back.

Lord Jackson walked over to Edwin and told him to keep a close eye on the old man. He then walked over to Sarah. He pulled her, Godwin, and the blacksmith into a huddle. "I don't get it. Everyone I ask has not had contact with anything or anyone in common."

The Blacksmith chimed in. "Except the well."

Sarah and Lord Jackson looked each other in the eyes. "The well!"

At that moment the cook delivered the bowl of stew to the old man. When he placed the stew on the table in front of him the old man's head flew back, his eyes rolled back into his head, and his body started to seizure. In an attempt to help the old man the cook tried to steady the old man's shoulders. As the old man's shaking subsided everyone was now on their toes with their swords at the ready.

The cook who was convinced the old man was going to be OK tried to convince the others. "He's fine. Look he stopped." he said as he stood with one hand across the old man's chest in an attempt to keep the others at bay.

"He is fine!" he repeated.

As the words left his mouth the old man leaned forward and took a big bite of flesh right out of the cooks arm. In an instant the cook let out a scream of pain that can only be compared to a young woman, but in a higher pitch. He fell to the floor clutching his arm as blood sprayed around him.

"He's not fine! He is definitely not fine!" the cook yelled out as he changed his mind completely.

The old man stood up with enough speed to knock over the table in front of him sending the bowl of stew flying thru the air. Lord Jackson without a second thought already set his sword in motion. The blade just missed the bowl as it flew thru the air and connected to the old man's neck separating his head from the rest of his body.

"Gabriel!" Emma yelled out.

The blacksmith stepped in front of Emma to shield her from the gruesome horror she had just witnessed. Bursting into tears she fought the blacksmiths hold for a slight moment then she relinquished control and buried her head into his arms.

Sarah noticed the cook was now starting to shake. Stepping up to the plate Sarah sent her sword crashing down thru the top of the cooks scull ceasing his movement completely.

Emma, without actually seeing it being done screamed out the word "No" into the blacksmiths shoulder and fell limp in his arms. He picked her up and carried her to the opposite side of the room.

Lord Jackson, wiped the blood from his blade. He noticed the terrified look on the other patrons faces. “Please, everyone stay calm.” he placed his sword back into its holster on his waist. “There is no need to panic. If we stay strong and keep together we will get thru this. I give you my word I will protect every single one of you. At all cost.”

Just then one of the boards from the window broke loose and five of the plagued from outside were now peeping in. Their hands started to push thru as they attempt to force themselves in. Quickly Edwin and Godwin start thrusting their swords thru the faces of the plagued. As one drops another quickly takes its place.

The Blacksmith and one of the patrons grabbed the fallen board and tried to get it back in to place. Edwin and Godwin are holding the creatures back as best they can. They tried to replace the board to its original spot but there were too many hands pushing thru. Edwin and Godwin never give up and hands were being cut to the floor. The plagued were finally pushed far enough back to finally place the board back in place. Edwin and Godwin took to the center of the board in order to hold it in place as the blacksmith and the patron started to nail it back into the frame. They grabbed additional wood to secure the window even more.

Edwin went to Lord Jackson “There numbers are increasing my lord. I do not know how much longer we will be safe here.”

The moans and the banging on the

outside were increasing. There getting louder and more intense. Lord Jackson looked to his men. “Has anyone checked the back? Is there a rear entrance?”

Sarah let him know “There is a back door. Emma and I have secured it. There was nothing out there last I looked. It seems they are all out front.”

“Godwin, you and Sarah go to the back and see what the situation looks like now.” Lord Jackson turned to the others. “The rest of you, I need you to rest and conserve your energy for if these things get in here we will need to move fast.”

Edwin turned to one of the patrons. “What is your name friend?”

“Eric” he replied.

“Thank you for helping with that window Eric. You showed a lot of courage helping with that. Thank you.”

Eric nodded his head and looked down in anguish.

Edwin placed pint of ale in front of Eric. Edwin then raised his pint to cheers, and took a giant swig. Wiping the beer from his upper lip he asked “What is your profession? “

“I work in the fields.” he said as he took a big swig of his own ale to calm his nerves.

“Good, that means you must know these fields around us pretty well then, right?”

“I do.”

“OK, so in that case if we needed to know the fastest way to get from here to the castle you could help me map it out. Right?”

Eric shook his head yes as his mouth was full of ale.

"Great." Edwin looked at another patron. "How about you. What is your name?"

"Robert."

"Robert, what is your profession?"

"I also work in the fields my lord."

"Very well. Why don't you come join Eric and me over here and we can come up with some form of an escape route. OK?"

The blacksmith took a rag from behind the bar and wet it. With it he walked over to Emma. He rung out the access water from the rag. He then took a seat next to her as she placed her hand on his leg he began to wipe her tear stained face. He ran his fingers through her hair not only to console her, but to also make sure her hair was not in her face. Knowing the pain she was feeling he vowed in his mind to be there for her, and to help her through this no matter what it took.

Sarah and Godwin came back to report. Sarah looked Lord Jackson in the eyes. "The back is secure. We did however see three of those things wondering in the back field."

Godwin added "If we exit out the back and stay to the right of the barn we should be able to get by them without detection."

Lord Jackson, Godwin and Sarah joined Edwin, Eric, and Robert at the table to establish a plan and a route back to the castle. With the plan and route secured Lord Jackson gathered everyone together.

"OK everyone, listen up. Here is the plan. We are all going to head out the back and head to the castle. We will be safe and secure behind the castle walls. Edwin will lead us. So make sure you follow him and stay close. Godwin will hold up the rear to make sure no one is left behind or lost. We need to move quickly and quietly. Whatever it takes. Do not get separated."

Emma spoke out "You are coming with us right?"

"Yes, I will be catching up to you all as soon as I know this place has been secured and you are all safely away. Now go. Everyone head out the back and stick together."

As the group headed out the back Sarah looked behind to see Lord Jackson pouring the ale on the floor. It hit her as to what his plan was and as she led the group out the back she decided to stays behind to help.

Lord Jackson caught his reflection in a mirror as he summoned his inner strength. He saw his eyes turn pitch black and his fangs protrude from his gums. In one swift moment he felt his senses heighten and started breaking up the barrels of ale so the ale covered the room. He stood by the front door with sword in hand and listened for any movement from the back. Not hearing a sound he figured they were all out and on their way. So with his sword he started to hack away at the boards just loosening them enough to let the plagued burst thru. As he saw the boards start to crack and give way he started to run towards the back door.

He saw Sarah standing in the doorway with a lantern in her hand. He smiled at her, and ran quickly to her side. Once he was at the door Sarah slammed the lantern to the floor setting the tavern a blaze along with all the creatures in it. Side by side they secured the back door and raced to catch up to the others.

Lord Jackson opened two giant wooden doors that lead to the study. Sarah walked into the room by his side. The room was quite dark. The only light illuminating the room was from a fireplace and two lanterns perched on the walls. The fire place was made of large stone slabs trimmed in heavy oak. Above the mantel hung the head of a lion who wore a terrifying grin. It seemed to have been cursed for all of eternity frozen in mid growl. Lord Jackson always thought it bore a striking resemblance to his father.

The blacksmith and Emma were snuggled up in the corner of the room wrapped in a quilt. Their eyes were closed as Emma's head rested upon his chest and his arms were wrapped around her tight.

The twins Edwin and Godwin were resting back to back next to the fire place. Eric and

Robert were each in a separate chairs. Everyone was completely passed out and in a peaceful deep sleep. The only sound heard was the crackling coming from the fireplace.

Not wanting to disturb them and there well needed slumber, Lord Jackson and Sarah both slowly backed out of the room. Lord Jackson gently closed the doors and as he let go of the handles he felt a tug at his jacket. He turned his head to find Jacob the boy he saved from the dockyard and took under his wing standing at his side.

"My lord..." Jacob started to say till he saw Lord Jackson raise his finger to his lips.

"Shh..." Lord Jackson interrupted.

"My Lord," Jacob started to whisper. "I have done what you asked. I offered to make everyone food as soon as they arrived, but once I came back to tell them it was ready they were all already fast asleep my lord."

"Thank you Jacob. You are indeed a fine help around here."

"Would you like me to fix you and Lady Sarah a plate to eat?"

"Oh Jacob you are a man above men." Sarah replied as she gave Jacob a kiss upon his cheek. "I would love nothing more."

"Yes, that sounds delightful," Lord Jackson replied as Jacob began to blush. "And please, be so kind as to bring it to my room when it's ready."

"Right away!" Jacob said. He quickly caught himself as he remembered to whisper. "My lord, my lady." Jacob bowed then turned and ran to the kitchen.

Lord Jackson led Sarah up the stair case to his bed chamber. As they reached his room he opened the door allowing her to enter the room first. She headed straight to his armoire where she saw an empty goblet. She pulled the goblet closer as she took a dagger from her belt. She raised her hand so that her wrist was directly above the goblet and she began to pierce her wrist with the dagger. The blood flowed into the goblet as she placed the dagger on the armoire. Once the goblet was full she wrapped a piece of cloth around her wrist. She then grabbed the goblet and turned to Lord Jackson.

Lord Jackson looked Sarah deep into her eyes and without a sound he grabbed her wrist and slowly removed the cloth. He gently raised her wrist directly to his mouth and began to feed. Without breaking his eye contact he took the goblet from her hand and placed it back to the armoire. He then placed his hand on the mid of her back. As he let go of her wrist she kept it firmly to his mouth. He reached his arm down around the back of her knees gently picking her up into his arms. He carried her to his bed. He laid her down and could see in her eyes that she was starting to weaken. He took her wrist from his mouth placing his thumb over the wound to stop the bleeding. With his other hand he tore a new piece of cloth from his beds canopy and wrapped it around her wrist.

Just as Lord Jackson finished tying the fabric securely around her wrist Sarah began to use her hands to undo the hinges of his vest. He allowed his vest to drop to the floor as he began to pull his shirt over the top of his head. Sarah sat up and started to kiss his stomach just above his bellybutton and her hands began to caress his chest.

Lord Jackson dropped his shirt to the floor and ran his hands down the middle of her back. Her forehead rested upon his stomach as he loosened up the lacing on the back of her dress. He could feel her lungs fill with air as he brought his hands back up to her neck. She looked up staring him in the eyes. His hands rested on her neck as he applied a slight bit of pressure for a few seconds then he began slowly running his hands down her shoulders causing the top of her dress to drop alongside his hands down to her elbows. He gently raked his fingernails slowly up her arms sending goosebumps all over her body.

Sarah slowly started to lick the left side of his stomach running the tip of her tongue over each muscle. Lord Jackson with a slight tug of her hair pulled her head back causing her mouth to open wide releasing a slight gasp for air. He leaned in closer and started to suck on her bottom lip.

Just as their mouths locked into an embrace they heard a knock at the door. They broke from there kiss. Paused for a moment. They rested forehead to forehead till they hear it again. Thump, thump, thump. Lord Jackson stood up straight and let out a sigh. Sarah fell back into the bed.

Jacob was standing in front of Lord Jackson's door with a tray of food in his hand. As he began to knock a third time the door opened. Lord

Jackson stood in the doorway and peered down at Jacob. Jacob began to hand Lord Jackson the tray of food when he looked into the room to see Sarah getting comfortable in bed. His eyes began to widen as he noticed that Sarah was bare chested. Lord Jackson realized what Jacob was bearing witness to, and decided to close the door slightly more cutting off Jacobs view.

Jacob blushed as he looked Lord Jackson in the eyes. “Here is your food my lord.”

Lord Jackson grabbed the tray from Jacob. “Thank you Jacob, that will be all for the night my friend.” he said with a smile.

“Goodnight my lord.”

“Goodnight.” he replied as he closed the door.

The next morning brought with it an orange glow that flooded the room. The glow beckoned Sarah’s eyes to open. She looked to her side to see Lord Jackson in a deep sleep with his arm wrapped around her waist. She laid still for just a moment and just looked at his peaceful somber face. She began to smile as she gently lifted his hand from her stomach. She gently eased herself out from the bed and placed his hand back onto the mattress. Still looking at his face she wanted to make sure he was not woken by her movement. She watched him mumble a tiny bit as he began to smile which brought warmth to her heart.

She leaned down and grabbed her undergarments and put them on as she walked over to the window sill. On her way she grabbed an apple from the tray of food that was brought last night. She opened the curtains just slightly trying not to let too much light into the room. She looked out of the window taking in the beautiful morning view, and took a bite out of the apple she grabbed. Just as she began to chew she noticed an older gentleman in a dark robe hobbling toward the front gate. He was carrying two large buckets filled with what looked to be water. She started to get a very uneasy feeling in her gut but she was not exactly sure why. Her natural curiosity grew as she quickly threw on the rest of her clothes. She quietly eased the door open and shut as she left the room in an attempt not to wake Lord Jackson.

She ran down the stairs as she fastened her corset. Thinking about what she had seen. It hit her that normally the buckets that the old man's was carrying would be empty if he was going out of the castle walls to fill them.

As she reached the front gates she saw no sign of the old man in the robe. Following her instincts she headed out of the front gates and headed straight to the nearest well.

She got about three quarters of the way there when she heard someone coming toward her. The morning sun was shining directly in her face so she was not sure if it was going to be the old man she was trying to follow or one of the creatures they have been encountering. She quickly jumped out of sight behind a tree. She quickly reached for her dagger and realized that it was not on her waist. She must have left it in Lord Jackson's room.

She heard the figure walk past on the

path. She turned to peek around the tree to see who or what it was walking by. She saw it was just the old man. She could also see that the buckets he was carrying were now empty. To get a better look she leaned out a bit and as she shifted her weight she heard a branch under her foot snap causing the old man to stop in his tracks.

Just before he was able to turn his head and look to see where the noise he heard came from Sarah ducked behind the tree once more. This time she made sure she was as quiet as she could be. The old man stood there listening for a moment. Listening for any other sounds. With an uneasy feeling in the pit of his stomach the old man coughed and continued on his way. This time with just a little bit more pep in his step.

Sarah stood there for a slight moment then decided the coast was clear. At that point she ran to the well that was just up ahead to look for anything out of the ordinary. She carefully looked at the well and its surroundings. Sarah could not see anything out of place. She decided to head back to the castle to let Lord Jackson know what she had seen.

She entered the front gates and saw Jacob gathering some fire wood. She scanned over the area around them. She then walked over to Jacob just to see if the old man was anywhere in sight.

She asked Jacob "Jacob, have you seen an old man in a robe pass thru here at any time the morning?"

"No my lady," Jacob replied "I just came out to get some fire wood so I can get breakfast started. You are the only person I have seen so far today my lady."

Sarah, slightly distracted from Jacobs' response stood there just looking around the courtyard.

"Is everything alright my lady?" Jacob asked as he stood there with his arms full of fire wood.

Sarah turned to him "Sorry Jacob, Yes I am fine. I have to run though. Save a plate for me later?"

"Of course my lady"

Jacob blushed when he remembered what he saw last night and began to smile. Sarah quickly ran back to Lord Jackson's room.

As she entered the room she could see Lord Jackson was still in a deep sleep. He was sprawled out across the bed with his bare ass to the wind. She paced back and forth as she debated in her head weather or not it was important enough to wake him. In mid pace she saw her dagger still in its sheath lying on the floor just next to the armoire. She bent down to retrieve it and she heard in a groggy voice.

"Good morning."

16

The horses where well fed, rested, and fully packed, ready for the long trip to Calais. The blacksmith held Emma close as they said their goodbyes. He held her head close to his chest and gently kissed her forehead.

"Do you have to go?" she asked.

"I do." he replied "They need me with them."

"I need you with me."

He held her face in his hands and looked deep into her eyes.

"I will be back as soon as I can." he said as he kissed her. "I need you to know I will return to be with you for the rest of our days. But I have to make sure we will still have a world worth living in when I return."

Edwin walked by smacking the

blacksmith on his ass.

"Break it up you two. We have to go soon."

Emma and the blacksmith tightened their embrace.

Edwin went horse to horse making sure everything was secure. He also tended to the cart with their supplies and equipment and made sure they are all secure as well.

Godwin walked up to the blacksmith and told him that it was time to go with a pat on the shoulder. Emma looked up at the blacksmiths face. He looked down at her then leaned down and kissed her lips once last time.

Lord Jackson and Sarah both walked out of the castle doors together. Lord Jackson had a stern yet determined look on his face and a strange bag was secured to his waist. They both walked straight to the horses. Without uttering a word he placed his foot into the stirrup and he threw his other leg over the horses back and started to ride to the gate.

Sarah and the others began to follow suite heading out right behind Lord Jackson. Jacob came out running to see them off. Emma and Jacob stood side by side and waved as they left. Jacob held his chest out tall making sure he looked them all in the eyes as they left. With that one look he intended to let them know he will be the man to take care of things while they are away.

The blacksmith was the last to ride out of the gate as they headed out. The Gate closed behind him. Jacob still standing tall wiped a single tear from his face. Emma tried her best not to cry. Instead she just messes up Jacobs hair as she walked him back inside.

17

The morning before they left for Calais, just as Lord Jackson awoke, Sarah told Lord Jackson what she encountered while he was asleep. Lord Jackson knew the man she had described. He was Sir Crowley, his father's medical and spiritual adviser, not to mention he was his father's personal barber as well. In fact he was also the head surgeon in charge of bloodletting and Lord Jackson knew just where to find him.

Lord Jackson got dressed and left his room. He headed straight down the hall with Sarah close behind. He first headed to the study. Once they got there Lord Jackson set one foot in the room and saw there was no one there. With a familiar scent in the air he knew just where to find the others. He headed straight to the kitchen.

Just as they reached the kitchen they ran

into Jacob who was carrying a tray of food.

"I was just bringing this to you my lord."

"Thank you Jacob." Lord Jackson replied as he grabbed a goblet and some bread from the tray. "I need you to tell the others that once there done eating they need to start getting the horses ready. I want to head out as soon as possible. OK?"

"Yes my lord. Right away."

Sarah grabbed some bread and fruit from the tray just as Jacob turned to head back to the others.

Lord Jackson continued down the hall, and Sarah continued to follow right behind him. They reached the far end of the castle. Lord Jackson grabbed a torch from the wall and started walking down a winding staircase. Sarah followed down the narrow winding staircase. She felt the air getting colder and colder the farther down they went. They finally reached the bottom of what seemed to be an endless stairway.

Lord Jackson lit the two lanterns affixed to the walls right at the end of the staircase. As they made their way down the corridor he lit a few more lanterns on their way. They got to the end of the corridor where it opened up revealing three doors. The doors on the right are large gated doors with extremely thick bars baring a massive lock in the center of each. To the left was a big wooden door appearing slightly larger than the other doors thru out the castle.

"Where are we?" Sarah inquired.

"That there," Lord Jackson replied pointing to the gated doors. "Leads to the dungeon. Trust me, you never want to be behind those gates.

Especially without the key."

"This here," he continued as he started to bang on the door to the left "Is where we are going to find..."

The door started to open as he pounded on it. Realizing the door was not locked his focus turned to entering the room.

Lord Jackson and Sarah were standing in what seemed to be a large laboratory. It was a large room and along the back wall they saw five large boxes covered in tarps. In the center of the room was a long table covered in quite a lot of papers, candles, and jars. In the center of the table was a large book surrounded by a bunch of used quills. To the right of the table hanging on the wall was a large board with straps. It was stained with multiple shades of blood from the top to the bottom.

Sarah cringed at the sight of it. She started remembering that the last time she saw that board it was being used at Lord Jackson's party.

"He doesn't seem to be here." Lord Jackson stated.

They both turned to leave when they heard a groan come from the back of the room. It stopped them both in their tracks. Lord Jackson started to investigate. Not quite sure where the sound was coming from exactly he headed straight to the back of the room and started to remove the tarp from one of the boxes.

Sarah's eyes widen with shock to see what she thought was going to be a crate was actually a cage. A second groan was heard and being the first cage was empty Lord Jackson began to remove the tarps from all five cages.

To their surprise one of the cages had a male figure curled up in the fetal position tucked away in the back corner of the cage. Dressed in rages he looked as if he had been there for months. They could barely see his face so they both got closer for a better look. Lord Jackson grabbed the lock with the intension to open the cage. The rattling of the cage caused the man to lash out on impulse. Biting and grabbing at Lord Jackson. They could both see the emptiness within the stranger's eyes and realized he was no longer human.

Not sure how or why this creature was down there they both took a step back. They looked each other in the eyes and heard the door shut behind them.

18

The summer heat has no mercy on the soldiers as they stand there guarding the front of Prince Edwards tent. Sweat continued to poor down there faces as they kept their poise and focus. Inside the tent they could hear the frustration pouring from the Princes mouth.

Inside of the tent is Prince Edward and his war council. They're standing around a table overlooking a map of the area. The unforgiving heat is making the worry on their faces transparent while the Princes anger grows to a point that with a mere glance, their minds are flushed of any and all ideas and replaced by fright.

"Stone, mortar, and wood! That is all that stands in my way, stone, mortar, and wood!" Prince Edward yells as he looks each and every one on his council in the eyes. "We have not found a way over it.

We have not found a way around it. We have certainly not found a way thru it or under it and I need to know why! Why is King Philip sitting comfortably inside those walls while I am stuck out here with you mindless bumbling idiots! Those are my walls! That is my castle! That is my throne and I am not going to stand by while his fat lazy ass is sitting in it!"

Everyone in the council lowers their eyes in shame as the prince continues.

"We have cannons, yes!? We have Catapults, Yes!? We even have ladders! Am I correct on this!?" he says as he grabs the collar of Lord Gerson who was unfortunately the closest person to him.

"Yes! Yes my lord! We do." he says in fear.

Prince Edward takes a deep breath in, and with a change of his demeanor from anger to disgust, he lets go of the man's collar and looks him straight into his eyes.

"Good, now let's find a way to use them." a slight moment passes as they all just stand there. "NOW!" he yells as he points to the door. "Find me a way to use them, NOW!"

Without missing a beat they all scatter out of the tent. Prince Edward retreats to the back of the tent and sits upon his chair. It's a big wooden chair with red velvet cushions. With one hand pinching the bridge of his nose just between his eyes his other hand reaches for his goblet perched on a table next to his chair.

As he raises the goblet to his mouth he can see it was empty. He lets the last drop inside drip out onto his tongue then tosses it across the room. He grabs a tiny bell from the table and begins to ring it. As the tent doors open he places the bell back on the table and two young women walk in and head straight to the Princes bed.

The Prince joins them on the bed sitting right in between the two. The woman on his left is a pale skinned redhead covered in freckles. The woman on his left is also pale skinned but she has long black hair and deep mysterious eyes.

With just a look from the prince the redhead starts to undo her clothing while the brunette starts to undo the Princes clothes. The dark haired vixen removes the prince's shirt and slowly runs her hands down his chest. He grabs both of the women by the hair on the back of their neck. He pulls the brunette's head closer to his mouth and starts to massage her neck with his tongue. While his other hand filled with red hair is pulled down between his legs. The redhead opens her mouth and begins to work her magic as he starts to get excited. As he is reaching his full level of excitement he pulls the dark haired vixens neck back even more and takes a bite. Blood trickles down her neck to her breast. After a minute or two he switches it up pulling the redhead up to his mouth for a bite and brings the brunettes head down entering her mouth.

19

Lord Jackson and Sarah both take a step back from what they just saw. They look each other in the eye and get startled when they hear the door close behind them. They turn to see Sir Crowley, an old man in a dark hooded cloak.

"Lord Jackson? Is that you? What are you two doing down here?" Crowley asks as he enters the room. He has a ring of keys tied to his waist and he is carrying a plate of food in his hand. Weary to get too close he scans the room. He can see the cages have been uncovered and a worried look falls upon his face.

"I think I should be the one asking questions here." Lord Jackson demands as he walks towards the man. "Who or what is this thing? And why do you have this thing here inside the castle?"

"I am not at liberty to discuss that with

you my lord." he replies as he shovels food into his mouth. "Your father..."

Lord Jackson draws his sword in anger and points it straight at the man's neck.

"My father? What does my father have to do with this?"

The old man swallows down the food in his mouth and replies cautiously "Your father has not given me permission to talk to anyone about this my lord."

"Permission? This is your permission right here." Lord Jackson says as he places the tip of the sword against the man's throat.

The man feels the tip of the blade on his Adams apple as he swallows. He contemplates the situation yet still breaks off a piece of bread and places it slowly into his mouth.

"Tell me what my father has to do with any of this."

The old man stays silent and continues to eat as Lord Jackson looks him deep into his eyes.

"Are you telling me my father has known about these things all this time?" He glances at Sarah with a look of disbelief. And in frustration swings his sword across the table knocking everything in its path to the floor including the old man's plate of food.

"It wasn't our intent for this to be the outcome you know. Your father just didn't understand that these things take time and time was something your father didn't give me enough of. He demands perfection, but this is what you get when you rush perfection." he says as he points to the thing in the cage.

"You created these things on purpose? What was my father thinking? And then to lie to my face as if he didn't know what I was talking about when I told him."

"We were trying to create a more viable and longer lasting food source. This was not our intent." Crowley pleads.

Sarah, stunned in silence can't believe what she is hearing and begins to cry.

"Not your intent?" Lord Jackson questions Crowley.

"No, my lord. We had good intentions. I just can't figure out what went wrong. We were attempting to give them a longer and stronger life. That way we would have a stronger and longer life."

Lord Jackson walks around the table with his head down dragging the tip of his sword along the floor. The weight of the sword causes the blade to mark the wood floor as he moves. He is stepping over and thru the rubble on the floor and as he stops directly in front of the old man he tightens his grip to the handle on his sword. He raises his head to look Crowley eye to eye.

"I guess I'll have to tell my father you failed." he says with a swing of his sword through Crowley's neck like a knife thru butter.

It's late in the evening and Prince Edwards tent is adorn with many lit candles. The rain drops hit the outside of the tent in a smooth calming pattern. Two women lay bare-skinned sprawled out in the blood stained bed while the prince also in the buff, sits at his desk contemplating his next movie.

With his legs crossed his elbow is perched on the desk as his hand runs through his hair. His other hand grasps the spine of his goblet as he pours the remaining contents into his mouth.

In frustration, the prince tosses the empty goblet across the room. The clatter it creates startles awake one of the women in the bed. She leans over to wake her friend to leave. With a nudge of her shoulder both girls slowly get up. Feeling drained and drowsy they grab there robes and leave.

The Blood of Royals

The Princes head now lays comfortably upon his forearms across the desk. He can feel the cool night air blow across the back of his neck as the entrance to the tent closes. The room lights up for a split second from the lightning outside, about ten seconds later a deep roar of thunder is heard. As the crack of the thunder dyes down Prince Edward can hear a faint whisper in the distant air yelling “Father!” Thru the rain drops he can hear the sound of horses closing in, and the word father is getting louder and louder.

Prince Edward has been eagerly awaiting his son’s arrival, so he quickly stands and puts on his robe. Hearing the halt of the horses he tightens his robe shut and stands tall to great his son.

Lord Jackson cautiously enters the tent securing the entrance shut as he takes a deep breath before he turns to confront his father.

“Ah Jackson my son, I am so glad to see you have finally come to join me in battle. Come, have a seat with me and we shall discus our victory plan.”

Lord Jackson, as his father sits and awaits his son to sit by his side, takes a good look around the room. Continuing to stand Lord Jackson looks his father deep into his eyes finally gathering the courage to say what he came there to say.

“How could you lie to me like you did? You sat there on your throne and acted like you had no clue as to what these things were. You pretended to know nothing about how they came about, how they were created. When you knew all along!”

Taken back by his son’s accusations the

Prince quickly turns to the defensive.

"How dare you speak to me in this manner? Have you forgotten that I am your father?"

"Have you forgotten that I am your son? You could have told me the truth."

"I have told you the truth, I have never once lied to you."

"Even now you're going to sit there and lie to my face and tell me you don't know how these things were created? I know the truth father. I know what you and that crazy old man did."

"Crazy old man? Do you mean Crowley?"

"Yes father, Crowley told me everything! How you were trying to create a more viable and longer lasting food source. And instead it created death and mayhem."

"Yes I had him working on something that would make our peasants stronger and live longer. So that way we would be able to stay well supplied in times like these, during wars like these. However he never told me anything went wrong. This is the first I am hearing of this. I had no clue that what he was doing was resulting in this. Jackson, I am not a monster. If I would have known I would have put a stop to this right away. My intentions were for the good of our people."

"Your intentions failed. And now our food source has diminished."

"That's it, I am going to have his head!"

Lord Jackson takes the bag from his waist and places it on his father's desk. The bag is wet and dripping in blood.

"No need." Lord Jackson says as he heads to exit the tent.

"Son, help me here. I am surrounded by morons. I can't win this without you. Help me win and we will clean all this up together."

"I'll sleep on it." he says as he exits the tent.

21

The morning wind blows cool from the rain that fell the night before. King Philip of France is perched safely upon the walls of his castle. With a mixture of stress and humidity the king uses his handkerchief made of the finest silk to wipe the consistent sweat from his brow. He gazes out among the vast ocean of soldiers below. With the current shipment of supplies arriving at this very moment King Philips mind eases just a bit knowing his kingdom will be safe for at least another two months. He knows his castle is virtually impenetrable and winning will come down to a giant waiting game as to who can hold out the longest.

In the loading docks the ships are docked secured and tied off. The king's soldiers begin to unload the ships as the sailors exit to recoup with food and drink.

The Blood of Royals

One of the king's soldiers begins to load a wooden cart with sacks of potatoes. He grabs one last sack to fill the cart and notices a young man in the corner hiding between two barrels. Thinking an enemy has stowed away to infiltrate the castle the soldier grabs the handle of his sword and walks closer to the young man. The closer he gets to the young man the more he realizes the man is just sick.

He holsters his sword and leans down to get a closer look. He sees the young man's eyes are rolled back into his head and his body is trembling. The soldier turns to shout for help and as soon as his head is turned the young man grabs the soldier by the shoulders and takes a bite right out of his neck. The soldier tries to scream but the damage to his neck inhibits his vocal chords. He reaches his hands behind his head in an attempt to stop the young man's attack. He grabs a hand full of hair and it rips right out of the young man's head. Without even a flinch the man continues to bite and tare the flesh from the soldier's body.

The king, from upon the wall, hears screaming coming from the courtyard. He immediately stands to check the front gate. He looks out amongst the field of English soldiers and sees no movement. The front gate appears to be intact. The king motions for his guard to go see what the commotion is all about.

A few minutes pass and the screams get louder and more intense. He starts to wonder why his guard has not come back to report the situation coming from the courtyard. King Philips curiosity gets the best of him as he heads down to the courtyard to investigate.

The Blood of Royals

The sounds get louder as he reaches the bottom of the stairs and as he stares out across the courtyard he can't believe his own eyes. He is standing witness to his own people attacking one another.

His eyes caught in a trance comes across a young girl five or six years of age leap over a barrel filled with hay to land on the back of a sailor running by. She takes a bite out of his shoulder blade which brings him to his knees and eventually laid out on the ground. She takes bite after bite as he his squirms to get away cease to persist.

An elderly woman is being chased by a couple of crazed eyed soldiers. She runs to a baby that was swaddled up laying on a haystack. She quickly grabs the baby into her arms and dips into a darkened corner. The soldiers that seemed to be chasing her pass her and the baby as if they were not even there. The soldiers actually being chased themselves run into the chapel closing the door behind them as the creature chasing them frantically tries to open it.

The king turning his attention back to the old lady to see if she and the child are OK. He begins to tear up when he sees the old woman unsuccessfully fight off two of the plagued who begin to feast on her and the baby.

King Philips senses are drowned out by the screams and the horrific sights that will now plague his mind for the rest of his life. His body is so numb with shock he fails to feel the bite being taken from his own calf. A young woman missing the lower half of her own body is laying on the floor chewing away.

The Blood of Royals

In front of the castle thru the field, an English soldier rides his horse at tops speed from the castle gates to Prince Edward's tent.

"Prince Edward!" the man yells out as he reaches the tent. As he dismounts his horse he is stopped by two guards.

"Prince Edward!" he yells again as he unsuccessfully tries to push his way past the guards. The prince exits the tent and as soon as he sees who the man is he motions for the guards to let him thru.

"My lord, you told me to let you know if there were any changes at the front gate."

"Correct." the prince replies. "What do you have to report?"

"My lord, all last night and most of today, up to just a few hours ago, most of us heard screaming come from inside the castle walls. Now just a few hours ago they all just seemed to stop. And once they stopped everything got really quiet. Eerily quiet my lord, to the point we didn't hear anything at all. As if the castle was abandoned. Some of us tried to get closer to find out what was going on, and that's when it happened my lord."

"What? What happened?

"The drawbridge my lord, the drawbridge begin to lower. I jumped on my horse that very second to come and bring you the news. It looks as if they might be surrendering."

"It's about time they have come to their senses! This is the greatest of news." the prince proclaims as he pats the man on the back. "We shall go

at once and welcome there surrender with open arms."
the prince looks around. "My son! Where is my son?"

22

The sky is dim. The amber glow of the sunset has dissipated into the night. The drawbridge is down, and Prince Edward sits tall upon his stead. On the Princes right hand side Lord Jackson has joined his father. Eagerly accompanied by Sarah, Edwin, Godwin, and the blacksmith. The Council is to the princes left and the entire English army stands behind them eagerly awaiting the French's surrender.

The Prince sent news to his father the King, of the surrender. Yet as he waits at an open drawbridge he start to wonder if he has sent word prematurely. Just at the point his anticipation turns to worry and just before the first bead of sweet even thinks of falling down his forehead, they start to see movement. Masses of people slowly start to exit from the castle, and the prince starts to welcome there surrender with a speech.

"With your peaceful surrender we now declare this land property of the king of England, King Edward the third..."

As Prince Edward continues his speech Lord Jackson starts to get an uneasy feeling in the pit of his stomach. He looks to his right and can see the joy on everyone's faces as they celebrate their victory. He catches Sarah's eyes as she smiles at him and she can immediately see the apprehensive look on his face. She knows right then and there that something is not right.

Lord Jackson tightens the horse's reins around his left hand as the horses start to get fidgety. His right hand clings tight to the handle of his sword. Thru the dark of the night the people emerging from the castle are not clearly seen. He squints his eyes to get a better look but, it's no help.

As the people get closer the Princes speech gets louder and the horses get more and more nervous. Torches are lit at each end of the drawbridge and as the people get closer there pace start to pick up. Lord Jackson locks eyes with one just as he passes by the torch and his fear is quickly realized. The lifeless gaze over the man's eyes are something he has seen many times at this point and his instinct kicks in causing his fangs to drop and his sword to breath.

"They've turned!" he yells out at the top of his lungs. And in the blink of an eye the crowed of people begin to attack. What Prince Edward anticipated to be a peaceful surrender is now a full-fledged blood bath.

Soldiers are either so shocked by what they are witnessing that they are becoming easy targets for these creatures to feast on, or they are overly frightened and killing anyone and everything around them. Lord Jackson's men branch out to cover more ground lobbing off head after head trying to gain control over the situation at hand.

Lord Jackson holds his ground on the front line. He looks to his left to see his father being tossed from his horse. Lord Jackson rushes to his father's aid. They grab each other's forearms as he lifts his father to his feet. Lord Jackson sees a creature running towards his father's back. He runs his sword thru the creatures head stopping it in its tracks. He quickly kicks the creatures limp body off of his sword.

Prince Edward leans into his son's ear asking "What is happening? What are these things?"

"These things are your creation father!" Lord Jackson replies. "This is what happens when you decide to play god! Looks like this curse you created has spread farther than I thought."

Prince Edward sees an elderly looking man running at him at full speed. The old man has that crazed look in his eyes and the prince runs his sword right thru the old man's chest, but he keeps reaching and biting at him as if nothing happened.

"Why won't you die!?" the Prince yells at the creature.

Lord Jackson drops his sword into the creatures head splitting it in half. The creature drops motionless and the prince pulls his sword from its chest. Lord Jackson looks sternly into his father's eyes.

"The head. Aim for the head." he tells his father as he continues to kill these creatures one by one.

The fighting goes on for hours, and hours. The sun starts to break thru the horizon. The persistence of the army prevails as it dwindles down the cursed to a mere few. Lord Jackson wipes the blood from his blade as he looks around for his crew. He spots a horse just a few feet away and as he mounts it he notices the blacksmith and Godwin. They're walking towards camp as he rides up next to them.

"Godwin, have either of you seen your brother or Sarah?

"There probably in camp celebrating already. As will we, once we get there that is."

Lord Jackson rides off ahead.

"Tell them to save some ale for us!" Godwin yells out to Lord Jackson as he goes. "They best not drink it all!"

As Lord Jackson rides off to camp he spots one of the cursed trapped under a wounded horse. He pulls his sword and as he rides by stabs the creature in the head putting it to rest and continues on to camp.

Lord Jackson makes it to camp and sees Edwin stumble out of a tent with an ale in his hands. Edwin sees Lord Jackson right away and starts to get excited.

"We did it brother!" Edwin yells out. "We came and we conquered my friend. Come. Come and celebrate with me. We will conquer our ale as we conquered those creatures!"

Lord Jackson hops down from the horse and grabs Edwin by his shoulders. "I will my friend, but first I need to find Sarah. Have you seen her? Is she here?"

"She is probably with my brother and what's his name, the blacksmith."

"No, I just ran into them on the way here. She wasn't with them."

Just then he sees Sarah down the path coming from his tent.

"There she is." Lord Jackson says as he pats Edwin on the shoulder. "Sarah!" he yells out to her.

Sarah turns to see Lord Jackson waiving for her to join him. Lord Jackson can see something is not right. Sarah has a deeply sad look upon her face as if she has been crying. Then she mounts her horse and starts to ride away.

Lord Jackson now extremely worried, quickly gets back on the horse and rides after her.

"Sarah wait!"

As he rides he quickly loses site of her, but he continues on following her trail. He gets about a mile outside of camp when he sees her horse tied to a tree. He dismounts his horse and ties it right next to hers.

"Sarah!?" he yells out. "Where are you? What's wrong? Whatever it is I can help. Where are you?"

He can see her foot prints leading to the east where he can also hear water flowing thru a creek. He walks thru the brush in that direction and sees her sitting on a rock crying. He walks up beside her.

"What's wrong?" he asks.

Not expecting to see him so soon she gets startled and jumps to her feet. She backs up a bit to stay clear from him.

"Please go back." she begs of him as she coughs into her hands. "You shouldn't be here. I don't want you to see me like this."

"See you like what? Are you hurt? What happened?" Lord Jackson asks as he steps closer.

Sarah raises her left hand to stop him as she coughs into her right. She slowly sits back down on some rocks and lifts her dress a bit to reveal her ankle. Lord Jackson can see the bite mark and feels his heart drop into his stomach. At that moment Sarah starts to cough so hard it causes her to pass out.

"No!" he cries out as he rushes to her side cradling her into his arms. "I won't let you die on me Sarah! I won't let you turn. I promise you."

Lord Jackson takes a bite out of his own wrist causing blood to expel from his veins. He holds it over her head allowing it to flow into her mouth.

"Please work." he says as he begins to bite into her wrist in an attempt to suck out the tainted blood as he replaces it with his own. He starts to get light headed and tries to fight it. As his sight grows dim he starts to recollect a time when he was younger. When he was a young boy in a cold classroom.

Lord Jackson has his head buried in his arms as he sits at a desk. The cool darkness is soothing to his eyes yet his relaxation is quickly interrupted by the loud sharp smacking sound of Baldric's switch hitting the desk. The sound causes his head to jump right up.

"Lord Jackson!" Baldric yells. "You may sleep on your own time but while you are in my care sleeping is strongly prohibited. We have a lot of ground to cover today, and this is very important."

Lord Jackson has a book directly in front of him on the desk. Baldric taps his switch on one of the pages.

"Please read aloud starting from here."

Lord Jackson takes a deep breath and starts to read.

"Mother Lilith has blessed us with life unlike all others. She will continue to bless us as long as our blood stays pure. Strigoi blood is to keep us pure. Our blood is strong and to contaminate or dilute it would be forbidden. Contamination of Strigoi blood can result in a corruption of life as it is known."

Lord Jackson pauses a bit to stare out the windowsill. Baldric smacks him in the shoulder with his switch.

"Continue!"

"All other blood both human and animal are simple in nature and is solely needed for nourishment. Strigoi blood is pure and strong and is what makes us who we are."

Baldric hits him in the shoulder with the switch.

"I haven't stopped!"

Lord Jackson feels the switch hit his shoulder again.

"Stop, OK. I'll keep reading!"

Smack...

Smack...

Smack...

Lord Jackson opens his eyes to see Edwin standing over him smacking him in the shoulder with a stick.

"There you are." Edwin says as he looks Lord Jackson in the eyes. "So, what are we reading?" he asks as he laughs. Edwin helps Lord Jackson to his feet.

Lord Jackson a bit out of sorts looks around. "Nothing. Where is Sarah? She was just right here."

"She is OK, Godwin brought her back to camp she said she felt tired and wanted to rest." Edwin replies.

"So she's alive?" Lord Jackson asks "She's not sick?"

"No she looked fine to me."

"Good, then let us head back to camp. I need to see for myself, I need to make sure she is OK." he says as he mounts his horse.

Lord Jackson enters his tent to see Sarah laying silently in his bed. He notices her body is not only covered in sweat but it has also been covered by every blanket found in the tent. It brings a calmness to his heart knowing she is in his care now. She is going to need time to rest and recover. Who better than Lord Jackson to make sure her transformation goes as smooth as possible?

He walks to the door of the tent and fastens it closed. He grabs a book from the desk and quietly pulls a chair close to the bed sitting beside Sarah. He takes his kerchief and wipes the sweat from her brow, he places the kerchief back into his pocket as he leans back and starts to read quietly to himself.

23

The sun caresses Sarah's naked body as she lays in a field of lilies. The lilies are a beautiful mixture of yellow, orange, and white. The aroma of each flower soothes her nostrils as she closes her eyes tight seeing nothing but the red of her eye lids as the sun attempts to break thru. Sarah's skin begins to feel goose bumps as the cool air blows across her bare skin.

Sarah's body begins to ease into a numbness she has never felt before where she no longer feels the heat nor the cold. She opens her eyes to see the sun set and begins to feel tiny pins and needles flow thru her body.

Air starts to flow across her back as her body starts to float into the air.

The feeling of weightlessness has rendered her body motionless. Her body is now floating just above the lilies and just as the sun finishes its descent into the ground around her the lilies turn to a deep dark red in color. Her body floats higher and higher into the air. The suns glow has now been replaced by the bright and inspiring lights reflection off of the moon. As the light of the moon hits her body it is as if it has blessed her skin for the first time. The warmth of the moonlight upon her body vanquishes any and all feeling of pins and needles she felt.

She has reached the top of the tree line and as the moonlight completely surrounds her she begins to regain control of her body. The helplessness she had felt as she was floating up into the sky has been replaced by a feeling like no other, a complete command of all her senses.

Sarah maneuvers herself into a standing position looking out across the field. In the farthest distance she sees a woman standing in the nude by a well. The lady is slim tall and her hair is dark and long almost touching the floor. The woman turns her head looking Sarah directly into her eyes beckoning for her to come closer.

With a whisper "Come closer my child. You need not fear me for I am apart of you and you are now a part of me."

Sarah floats down to her in what seems to take an instant as if distance no longer existed. Now, standing in front of the lady Sarah asks "Who are you?"

"I go by many names for I am the mother of us all and I am all that I am mother to. Do you understand?"

"Yes." Sarah replies.

"Just as many before you have, you may call me Lilith." she states with a slight curtsy and grin.

"Lilith, am I dreaming?"

"No, my dear Sarah." Lilith answers as she puts her arm around her. "Dreams are nothing but your unconsciousness viewing visions from your souls past and the future all at once. What you see in your dreams are what your mind is able to comprehend of the visions at that time. What you are experiencing now is not a dream it's an awakening of your soul. Up until this moment your soul has been in a prison of sorts jumping from body to body when it's able. When death and life collide allowing it to transfer from one body to another. And yet now your body and soul have finally been able to truly connect. Our blood is that key Sarah. It is the key that releases our souls to be free and allows us true control over our selves and true control over our own souls. Let me ask you this. Do you feel like your dreaming or do you feel awake?"

"I feel more awake now than I have ever felt in my life."

Lilith leads Sarah to a sweet little cottage where they walk inside to a kitchen. The kitchen is something Sarah has never seen before. So many devices and textures she has never encountered. It looked as if it was plucked from a sears catalog from the 1950's in a simple green and white motif.

Once in the kitchen Lilith now adorns a typical outfit suitable of a 50's housewife and Sarah in a 50's schoolgirl outfit poodle skirt and all. Lilith pulls out a chair for Sarah to sit and begins to pull cups from a cabinet.

"Oh to feel this all for the first time again, how I would die to be in your shoes right now."

Sarah looks down to see two shiny black and white saddle shoes upon her feet. Tapping them together to get a better feel. She smiles with curiosity.

"I envy you. You must have a million questions rolling around in that head of yours. Please I am here to answer what I can." Lilith tells Sarah as she makes her a cup of coffee.

"What is this place?" she asks.

"Ah yes. This is a kitchen. And this here is called coffee." as Lilith hands a cup to Sarah. "You drink it, but be careful it is quite hot. It is one of the best things the future has in store for us. Amongst many other delights you will encounter within your life. If you are careful Sarah you will get to see it all."

Sarah blows on the coffee and takes a sip. A grin forms on her face that runs from ear to ear.

Lilith chuckles "I told you."

"If this is what the future holds life will be good indeed." Sarah states.

"Yes, life will definitely have its ups but, it will also have its downs. The key is to not let the downs outweigh the good in life no matter how bad life gets always remember Coffee is on its way."

Sarah takes a deep breath in not only taking in the advice Lilith has just given her but filling her pallet with the warm aroma from the coffee in front of her. She takes another sip contemplating her next question.

Both Sarah and Lilith sit and talk in that kitchen discussing life, love, death, and countless other topics for what seemed to be hours and hours on end. They laugh a bit they cry a bit they even let themselves sit in silence for a bit to take everything in. Once they were done Lilith walked Sarah to the door she opened it and told Sarah she could come and talk to her at any time. They embrace each other and say their goodbyes. Sarah walks out of the door with her head held high feeling good not only about herself but about her future to come. Lilith closes the door behind her and smiles.

Sarah opens her eyes, slowly taking in her surroundings. She slowly removes some of the blankets that lay upon her body as she sits up in the bed. She sees Lord Jackson next to her sitting in a chair fast asleep with an open book in his lap and about 6 others closed by his feet.

Sarah sees his left hand on the edge of the arm of the chair and places her hand upon his. Feeling her soft hand caressing his own he opens his eyes to see her awake and smiling. He placed the book from his lap to the floor. He places his hand on top of hers and smiles back.

"Welcome back, how do you feel?" he asks as he hands her a goblet to drink from.

She quickly drinks from the cup, and tosses it to the ground. They both stand and embrace each other as tightly as they can.

"I feel so much better than I have ever felt before."

"One week, you were out for one week." Lord Jackson starts to explain to Sarah as they get there horses ready to ride back home.

Sarah draped from head to toe with blankets to hide herself from the sun starts to mount her horse.

"It didn't seem that long. Are you sure? And why is it I am so sensitive to the sunlight now? I'm so hot even under these blankets my skin feels on fire."

"Yeah that? That's temporary, it will get easier. Think of it like this. You know how your eyes have to adjust to the light when you first wake or if you have been in the dark for a long time? Well with your soul it's the same concept. Your soul has been trapped in the dark for most of your life and it may take some time for it to get used to the light. That's why we have our ceremonies at such a young age to reduce the recovery time. I was out for five days so you being out for only a week is not so bad. You should be able to adjust in just a few weeks. Here, keep hydrated. It will help." he says as he hands her a pouch.

Sarah takes a sip and can't believe how quenching it is. Her body is filled with such energy and strength. She never thought a pouch of blood could be so refreshing.

The horses are all loaded and ready to ride. Edwin and Godwin start to ride up front. Lord Jackson rides alongside Sarah as the blacksmith holds the rear. As they ride about a mile down the road it seems to be eerily empty. Up ahead Godwin notices a rustling in the woods so he raises his hand in a fist and starts to slow. The group rides closer and tighter together to prepare for whatever might be lurking ahead. They all have one hand griping their swords as there other holds tight to the rains.

The rustling ahead is now only about a few feet away. The rustling gets louder as they see two young kids plow onto the road wrestling with each other and laughing out loud. They both look to be about twelve or thirteen in age both in torn a ratted clothes covered in dirt. Edwin's horse releases a snort stopping the kids in their tracks.

"So sorry my lord." one of the kids starts to apologize. "We didn't realize you were there."

"Yes, so sorry my lord. We were just playing around." the other kids adds.

"Have no fear from us, for we are just

passing thru." Godwin says to ease the kid's worries. "Though, tell me. Have you seen anything out of the ordinary in the past couple of days around here?"

"No sire, everything has been quite normal I'd say." one kid says.

"How about any illnesses? Do you know or have you seen anyone who might be sick or injured?"

"No my lord, not in quite some time. Are you a healer?"

"Not quite kid. Thanks" Godwin says as he tosses the kids a few coins from his pocket.

The kids quickly pick up the coins and run off as the group starts to ride off again. The butcher rides up closer to Lord Jackson.

"Do you think this is the end? Do you think it's finally over?" the blacksmith asks.

"I hope so, but honestly I don't know. Let's just get back home and regroup. I'm sure we will find out sooner or later."

"Agreed." the blacksmith says as he takes up the rear again.

Edwin looks back at Lord Jackson seeing him tend to Sarah making sure she's feeling alright. Edwin then looks his brother in the eye and without saying a word they both nod in agreement then go back to looking out ahead.

As Lord Jackson holds himself up in his tent with Sarah one week prior. Edwin Godwin and the blacksmith start to help with the cleanup. As they pile body on top of body they set each pile a fire in hopes to purify the contaminated. Any and all swords and shields they find are collected and brought to the newly seized castle of Calais for cleaning and storage.

After a day in the field Edwin and Godwin decide to make their way into the newly acquired castle to see if they can be of any help to the prince. As they get closer to the castle they see wheelbarrow after wheelbarrow of bodies still being removed from the inside the castle walls. They notice the bodies are being lined up around the outer rim of the castle moat.

Once in the castle they see soldier after

soldier cleaning what they can. They notice a sign hanging from one of the doors that simply showed a barrel with the word ale in its center. They look each other in the eye and nod as they walk into the tavern. They were quite surprised at how empty the place was. They both look around Edwin finds two empty goblets and starts to fill them with ale and Godwin turns upright a couple of chairs and a table. They both sit, clink there goblets in the air, and take a huge gulp. Edwin sits back in his chair and rubs the back of his neck. Godwin hunches forward with his arms resting on the table goblet in hand and lets out a sigh.

"You said it brother." Edwin proclaims. "I am exhausted beyond comprehension. I am even too tired to complain about this shit French ale."

They both laugh as they poor more ale down their throats.

"Do you think he did the right thing?" Godwin asks his brother.

"I think he did what he had to do, or what he thought he had to do. Do I think it was right though? I don't know." Edwin replies.

"Now don't get me wrong I love Sarah as if she was my own sister but we both know she was not born into our blood line." Godwin states. "What if his actions curse us all? What then?"

"I don't know."

A noise is heard just outside the tavern causing the brothers to halt in conversation. They both take a moment and survey their surroundings. Two men walk by the outside of the window dragging something behind them. After a few minutes all went back to silence. Both brothers come to the conclusion that all is well.

"We need to tell the Prince." Godwin suggests.

"I am not so sure that is the best idea either. He is the one who put us in this mess in the first place."

Godwin gets up to get refills. "We need to tell somebody. We need to know what will become of all this."

"I tell you what, once she awakens we will have her tested."

"Do you mean?"

"Yes, once she's awake Lord Jackson will want to head home. Before that happens one of us will need to break away to enlist the services of Sir Nicolas Flamel. We can have him meet us at the castle. He is the only one I can think of that can bring light to our situation."

"Of course, Flamel. You're right. If anyone will know he will. Do we tell Lord Jackson?"

"No!" Edwin states adamantly. "I want to see where his loyalty lies. His heart might be clouding his vision, and if that's true then he is going to need to make a choice between us and her."

"Agreed, what do we tell Prince Edward?"

"Well there is no need to involve him at the moment. Let him enjoy his win for now. Besides this war is far from over and until we know where Lord

Jacksons head is at we might just need him a little bit longer."

The brothers clink there goblets together and down there ales. Just as they place the goblets on the table and lean back to finally relax a bit. The tavern doors open and in walks the blacksmith.

"How did I know I would find the two of you here? Please just tell me you left at least a small drop for yours truly."

Just then they hear the bell tower ring. All three men make their way to the castle wall just in time to see one of the princes archers let loose an arrow engulfed in flame. The arrow soars thru the air and makes contact with one of the bodies that aligned the outside of the castle moat. The flames spread quickly and caused the bodies circling the castle to be lit up like never before. The three of them looked in amazement as they stood there surrounded by a burning ring of fire.

A campfire crackles with a mist of yellow and orange flames releasing a mild yet comforting smoke in to the air. The glow from the fire slowly dies down as the night air begins to cool. All that is heard in the night air is the sound of crickets chirping as the crew lay asleep.

Lord Jackson lays with his chest along Sarah's back to keep her warm. His arm is wrapped around her waist for comfort. His nose is snuggled into her neck for his peace of mind. They all lay around the fire as Edwin takes first watch.

Godwin sneaks away to acquire Nicolas Flamel the one and only man they feel who has the answers to all of their questions. He heads out as quiet as he can not to disturb Lord Jackson and the others as they sleep.

Edwin sits on a log just next to the

blacksmith as he lays asleep. Edwin looks up at the stars with an appreciation he has never had before. The weight of the situation that is to come and of what has been already bears down on his chest and brings a single tear to his left eye. He quickly wipes it from his cheek and looks around to see if anyone bore witness.

Edwin notices the blacksmith starts to squirm and mumble. Before the mumbling gets louder and he ends up waking everyone up, Edwin taps his foot on the blacksmiths forehead. With one tap of his boot the blacksmith jolts awake in a panic.

Edwin shushes the blacksmith as he sits up in a cold sweat.

The blacksmith whispers "What time is it?"

"It's still late. You must have been having some kind of dream their brother."

"Killian." The blacksmith replies.

"What?" Edwin says in confusion.

"My name. My name is Killian." He responds.

Edwin looks at him a bit confused. Killian laughs a bit.

"For some reason you never call me by my name. Why is that?"

"Oh please, do not take offence." Edwin says "I never call anyone by their name. That's just me. Faces I remember, names I do not."

"No worries." Killian responds.

"So Killian," Edwin questions "What was with that dream of yours? It looked intense."

Killian replies "I honestly don't remember."

At that moment a snap of a branch is herd. Then shortly followed by a rustle in the bushes. Both men jump to their feet. Swords drawn. Tips pointed in the direction of the sound. They start to hear more rustling as it slowly surrounds them.

Killian steps back and nudges the back of his heal into Lord Jackson's side nudging him awake. Lord Jackson sits up and notices both Edwin and Killian up looking around with their swords drawn. Lord Jackson sniffs the air and slowly pulls his sword from its sheath.

Nudging Sarah awake, he says in a whisper "They're here."

At that moment a skulk of foxes stormed from the bushes jumping and running until they noticed Lord Jackson and his crew which caused them to stop dead in their tracks.

The group all let out a sigh of relief as the tips of their swords fall to the ground. The sound makes the skulk of foxes begin to scurry again jumping and running around. Sarah attempts to grab one and to play as it twist and turns in an evasive manner running swiftly away. The foxes continue on their way.

Not quite sure how to process what has just occurred the group looks at each other and begin to laugh. Killian, chuckling as he sits, plops down on a log and as his laughing subsides he glances to his left to see the torso of one of those creatures with no legs crawling onto the log. With a high pitch girlish scream and a burst of energy he jumps to his feet. Swatting his sword down creatures head smashing it to pieces upon the log.

High pitched screaming turned into angry forceful grunts. His arms get heavier with each swing as the creatures head is pulverized until it looks more and more like apple sauce. His sword comes to a halt as he turns his head to see everyone staring in confusion. He wipes the sweat from his brow and shrugs as he points to what was once one of the plagued and gives a smile. The rest of the group gets a chill down there spines as they grip the handles of their swords just a bit tighter than before.

27

September 12th, 1344

Today my love and the others head out to Calais. It has been 10 years since I lost my parents and five months since I lost my families tavern. Please don't let me lose Killian as well. The moment I met him I just knew there was something there, something more than I have ever felt before. Dear god, I pray to thee to bring him back to me safe and sound. I realize it has only been a short time but, I pledge my dedication to him. I must stay strong for him and, I must stay strong for Jacob. Instead of filling my head with wondering thoughts of what might cause my Killian not to return to me. I will dedicate my faith in you oh lord and trust you will bring him back home to my arms where he belongs.

I swear will focus on the survival of this place to make sure they have a home to return to. There is a lot of work to do and I will get it done. Jacob is strong and willing but I know he is still yet a child. He has not spoken much of his past and what happened to his family, but I will care for him as if he was my own. Lord knows I have yet to bare any children of my own, but god willing I will raise the family he provides.

The Blood of Royals

September 15th, 1344

This morning Jacob and I have gathered all the townsfolk we could find that have survived this horrible ordeal. We have counted 25 so far. I have made an attempt to try and ease everyone's minds by letting them all stay within the castle walls for safety.

Every day going forward I will delegate chores and projects to keep everyone busy so there is no time for them to think of the losses they have endured. To prevent any further outbreaks we have found that boiling the water be for we use it seems to be killing off whatever is causing the contamination. It seems to be working well and we have been able to use it for drinking water again. We are making great use of what we have, and I plan on having a life worth living again even if it kills me. I know it is going to take a lot of hard work and sacrifice on all of our parts but I feel we shall get thru this together.

A search party will be formed each day to go out and find survivors. I am not sure if anybody truly knows how far this epidemic has spread, the lengths it has reached, but we will do our best to make sure that there is no man, woman, or child left behind.

Tonight, to boost morale and ease our dark thoughts we will have a feast full of food and drink. I will make a full attempt to keep a steady brewing of ale so we can have a nightly celebration of life. I figure such a gathering will remind us that life is still among us and with gods will it will be for quite some time.

The Blood of Royals

September 28th, 1344

Today has been a quiet day with no sight of any of those creatures. Hopefully it is the mark of the end of all this chaos. I can only pray that this is the last anyone will see of these things, these creatures.

I learned these past weeks that Jacob is quite the cook. This morning he was awake and in the kitchen way before I was even out of bed. He made me the most wonderful fruit tart for breakfast. It was quite delectable. I think tomorrow I will teach him the secret to my mother's pie crust.

Last night was on the chilly side so today I ventured out on my own to collect some fire wood for the first time. It took me some time but I got the hang of it quickly. Though as I was just about done I heard a rustling in the trees, but it was just a squirrel. I was ready though with my axe in hand I stood my ground. My love would be so proud. Though none the less it was just a squirrel.

The Blood of Royals

October 10th, 1344

I awoke startled this morning by a loud crashing noise coming from outside my window. I ran to see what the commotion was and I could see the horses in the stable trying to break free. Bucking and kicking at the gates it was obvious something had them spooked. I quickly dressed and headed out to the stables to see what was going on. As I made it outside I noticed Jacob standing near the front gate. I called out to him with no response he didn't move a muscle. It didn't take me long to see why.

The front gate was rattling. There was no knock or cry to be let in, but just a rattling. I looked at the trees and there was no movement. The wind was calm. In fact it was eerily calm. I found myself standing and staring at the door just as Jacob was. Just then a fly flew past my ear. I heard the buzzing of its wing and it sent a chill across my body.

At that moment I decided to get a bit closer to see if I could hear anything, anything at all. My legs didn't move as quickly as they normally do and as I got closer and closer every tiny noise I heard sent more and more chills across my body and down my spine. Then all at once the chills stopped as I heard a single grunt come from the other side of the gate. A deep long grunt, and as quickly as I heard it my fear turned to action. I turned and grabbed Jacob by the arm. I told him to grab as much fire wood as he could and bring it to the top of the wall. I had an idea.

Once I was at the top I looked over the edge and I saw about fifteen maybe twenty of those creatures. There are also two giant pots just above the gate that are always filled with tar for just this type of occasion. We quickly set fires beneath both pots and calmly waited for them to boil. Once they were ready I gave the command. The pots were rigged with a lever, with Jacob on one lever I grabbed the other and as we pulled down we watched as the tar poured right out of each pot landing on the creatures below.

As the boiling tar poured over their heads there grunts ceased and their bodies seemed to just fall to the ground. I noticed there were no screams or cries for help. There was no squirming or running to get away. They all just accepted their fate and dropped to the ground. At that moment everything I refused to feel, everything I pushed back and hidden deep inside of myself, all of these terrified emotions came flooding to the surface. My eyes filled with tears and my body collapsed to the ground. I cried with such relief I sat back against the wall and just let everything out.

The Blood of Royals

Jacob tried his best to comfort me but my head was swimming. I couldn't make out what he was trying to say. Once the tears subsided a bit and I could start to see again my focus came back to Jacob who was yelling at this point. He was screaming asking me if I knew how to use a bow. I immediately thought back to my child hood and how my father taught me how to hunt with a bow. So I told him I did and asked him why. He looked over the wall and pointed at something. I got up and saw two straggling creature walking out of the forest thru the field.

I quickly grabbed the bow from Jacob's hands and lined up my shot. I lined up with the closest creatures head and as soon as I saw its eyes which seemed to stair directly into mine, I let go. The arrow flew fast and direct and got the creature right in the forehead. As it pierced through the flesh, the creature quickly dropped to the ground. The second shot went straight into the chest of the second creature and I could not believe it was still moving forward getting closer and closer. I grabbed a third arrow and took a moment to breath. I could hear my father in the back of my head telling me not to rush, to take my time and focus on the eyes. So I waited for my shot, and there it was. I felt the bow string flee from my finger tips and watched the arrow slice thru the air with ease piercing the creature right thru the left eye socket. A gleam of pride poured over me as I hear my father's voice saying how proud he is of me for that beautiful shot.

The Blood of Royals

November 9th, 1344

I woke this morning and my head felt like it was splitting itself right down the center. My worry for the others is now causing me physical pain. Though there has been no sign of the creatures in roughly four weeks, I feel they could still be out there just watching us. I can't help but feel they are going to return at any moment. They continue to haunt my dreams. My nerves are so shot that my whole body just feels weak. I had no intension of leaving the bed today, so this morning I tried to distract myself with kinder and gentler thoughts.

My mind turned to Killian. Oh how I miss him so much. I miss the warmth of his hands and the comfort of his embrace. I miss his scent. It was the scent of a real man. The way he looks at me. The way he touches me. As I keep thinking of him I could feel my stomach start to quiver. So I decided to get a bit more comfortable.

And that's when I heard it. Someone knocking at my door. In frustration I grab a pillow throwing it over my face as I scream as loud as I could. Knock. Knock. Knock. It wouldn't stop.

I yelled out, knowing it could only be Jacob, asking what it is he wanted. What he replied brought me strait to my feet and a smile on my face. Five beautiful words came shining thru that door. Someone-is-at-the-gate. I told him I was on my way as I quickly thru something on.

As I reached the gate Jacob was ready and waiting to open it. I stood there in anticipation ready to great whoever it was on the other side. My palms were sweaty silently praying to God above for it to be Killian and the others.

Jacob started to open the gate and I could barely make out two figures on horseback. As they got closer I quickly recognized Godwin witch immediately put a smile on my face. The other man is someone I have never seen before. He was a much older gentleman. Godwin dismounted his horse handing the reigns to Jacob and helped the old man down from his. I quickly ran over to Godwin throwing my arms around his neck. I whispered into his ear asking "Where are the others?"

Killian's hands are soar from holding tight to the reins for what seemed to be an eternity. His eyes sting as the sweat beads down his forehead causing his vision to blur. His hand fills with sharp pain as he releases the reign a bit to wipe the sweat from his brow and eyes. Looking forward he can see the others are just as beet, just as tired.

Sarah seemed to be the exception. She was wide awake and full of energy. Every little thing grabbed her attention as if she was a child experiencing life for the first time. As familiar as the terrain was getting the exhaustion seemed to blind the others as they arrived closer to home.

Killian's ears perk up when he hears Sarah speak up.

"I know that well. Look Jackson, it's our

well."

Those words sent a bolt of electricity shooting thru Killian's body. Dissipating any and all exhaustion the trip home has pounded into his being. He begins to ride like the wind. As he passes the others his energy is contagious waking there spirits. Everyone's eyes get big and they begin to ride faster.

Killian is the first to reach the gate. He jumps down from his horse faster than the horse can stop. He runs to the door knocking as hard as he can.

"We're back, baby we are back! Quick let us in!" He yells from the top of his lungs as he knocks harder and harder. The door begins to open and what seems to be in slow motion he sees his one and only true love.

Emma walks straight toward her man with her hair flowing in the wind and her arms reaching out to him. As soon as the door opens enough for him to squeeze thru he runs to her grabbing her by the waste and lifting her high into the air. He spins her in the air and gently lowers her down where their bodies are level. He leans in ever so gently looking her deep in the eyes and kisses her lips. There embrace tightens as they hold each other closer and closer.

Edwin walks past smacking Killian on his ass while he say "OK, you two. Now bring her upstairs and give her a proper welcome home. My brother should be arriving soon with a bit of a surprise."

Emma pulls away from Killian's kiss for a moment to tell Edwin "Godwin has already arrived my lord. He and his guest are waiting for everyone inside."

"Hmm." Edwin replies, as Emma takes Killian's hand and leads him upstairs.

Edwin walks over to Lord Jackson as he's handing off his horse to Jacob. "Make sure he is well feed and has plenty of clean water." Lord Jackson tells Jacob.

"My lord, I need to speak to you before we go inside." Edwin starts as he puts his arm around Lord Jackson's shoulders. "You see,
Godwin and I thought it would be helpful if we brought someone who can not only help us assess the situation, but also someone who can help Sarah with what she is going through as well."

Lord Jackson looks into Edwin's eyes with a stern glance, "Who?"

"Sir Robert Flamel, My lord." Edwin replies. "Godwin set off to retrieve him because we thought he would help make sense of all that is going on."

Lord Jackson grabs Edwin by the back of the neck and pulls him close. "Look, I understand why you did what you did. And I actually agree we need some answers. But..." Lord Jackson tightens his grip. "Never. I mean it. Never go behind my back again! Brother, we need to have faith in each other. Otherwise what are we doing here? Come on brother..." Lord Jackson changes his grip into a hug. "I Love you. Let's go get some ale. I'm parched."

Godwin greets everyone as they come thru the door. Edwin and Lord Jackson are the last to walk in. Godwin walks over slightly tipsy and wedges himself in between the two. "I love you guys. You two are absolutely the best friends a guy can ask for. And do I have a surprise for you."

"I told him about Flamel already brother." Edwin proclaims.

"Really," Godwin says in disgust. Godwin turns to Lord Jackson. "Well, looks like you, and only you are the best friend a guy can ask for. Now right this way gentleman and ladies."

Godwin leads everyone down stairs to the laboratory. As they enter Flamel walks over to Sarah. He grabs her by the shoulders and takes a deep breath sniffing the air close to her head. He takes her hand and leads her to the table in the middle of the room. "It's you isn't it? I can tell by your sent. Its new, it's so soft and gentle. It's like nothing I have ever smelled before. It's quite beautiful. May I see your hand please?"

"What? Why?" Sarah asks as her hand is pulled in close to Flamel. Just before she can utter another syllable Flamel pricks her finger and squeezes a few drops of her blood into a tube.

Flamel can see everyone's eyes bearing down on him as he works. He adds something into the tube that starts bubbling and changing colors as it mixes with Sarah's blood. He sets it down, and hands Sarah a wet cloth to wipe off her finger.

"As you all may or may not know..." Flamel starts. "Lilith was Gods first attempt at human life. She was created not only in Gods image, but in Gods image of perfection. She embodied everything

God loved and adored. Created directly from the twinkle in Gods eye. He could see after a while she was growing lonely so he created man in his own image to keep her company in a way he could not. And he was called Adam. For a long time they lived happily in the Garden of Eden. But as time went on Adam grew more and more controlling of Lilith which did not please God one bit. One day Adam went too far and laid his hands upon her in anger. God decided he has had enough, and for her protection God released her from the Garden allowing her to be free from any and all restrictions. Releasing her from the burdens of human life. As Adams punishment God decides to remove one of Adam's ribs and told Adam he was to spend life in the Garden of Eden alone for eternity. Adam begged and pleaded with God proclaiming his undying devotion and his eternal remorse for what he has done. God decided to give Adam one more chance. With the rib he took from Adam he created Eve. Being Lilith was created from the twinkle in Gods eye and no one could have taken her place. He created Eve from the twinkle in Adams eye. What God did not expect was how this would make Lilith feel. God never imagined the depth of jealousy that would scorn through Lilith's mind. She didn't see her release from Eden as freedom she saw it as a banishment. She felt betrayed by the one person she never thought could make her feel that way. Then when she found out she was replaced by Eve she became furious. Lilith knew the one rule that God gave to the Garden. It was his one test of faith and devotion. The apple.

Lilith knew Adam would not bend so easily, so she set her sights on Eve. Being Lilith was no longer bound to the same limitations that Adam and Eve were, she chose a disguise and went to work.

I am sure you know the rest of the story Eve ate the apple, and Adam blinded by love followed suite. Blah blah blah…" Flamel looks at the tube and pours it out onto the table where it starts to harden he quickly covers it with a cool rage.

"What people don't know is…" Flamel continues. "That God also punished Lilith. He cursed her with an unquenchable thirst. It wasn't for a great many years till she found out the one thing that would finally quench her thirst was human blood, and even more years later till she found out her blood was transferable, and she was able to create us in her likeness. Though with each new strand that is created there is a level of delusion that accurse but at the same time there is a core to the strand that certain elements do remain. And when the blood is combined with this. A mixture of my creation it tends to create something beautiful." He lifts the rag from what was poured out on the table.

Everyone in the room is in aww. Their eyes are wide and their jaws are dropped. Godwin in a slightly enamored state blurts out "Is that gold?" the room remains quiet. And Flamel starts to chuckle. "Cause that sure as hell looks like gold to me."

"Yes. Godwin that is exactly what it is." Flamel responds.

Lord Jackson picks it up slowly. Looking

it over extremely carefully. "Wow." He proclaims. "You must be one wealthy man Sir Flamel."

"Sadly no, Lord Jackson. See there is a catch to making this work. There must be an agent in the mix that will unlock the bloods elements and the only thing I know that can do that is a spice found in the Italian region called garlic. And we are all highly allergic to it. One false move and it can bring death upon its handler."

Lord Jackson whispers something into Flamel's ears.

"Of course, for you my Lord, anything." Flamel replies.

Lord Jackson turns to everyone in the room. "Alright, let us all retreat to the dining hall for some well over do food and ale. We are finally home and this calls for a grand celebration!" Lord Jackson swings one arm over Flamel's shoulders and the other arm around Sarah's as they head upstairs.

At the head table Sarah sits to Lord Jackson's right and Flamel sits to his left. In front of them on the table was an amazing spread of meats, fruits, breads, and cheeses. Everyone around the table is laughing and having a great time. In the midst of it all Flamel leans over to Lord Jackson and whispers to him.

"M' Lord when you get a chance may I speak to you in private?"

"Of course, we will soon." Lord Jackson replies. As he leans back to reflect on how amazed he is, and that all his friends are here laughing and having a good time. He takes a bite out of his apple and smiles.

29

Lord Jackson walks down the stairs toward the laboratory to meet with Flamel. He pounds on the door. Yelling "Flamel!"

He pounds on the door again, and it starts to crack open. As he pushes his way in he starts his spiel.

"Flamel, I am sure you have seen these creatures that have been spreading like wild fire and destroying everything in sight. Right?" Lord Jackson states as he works his way thru the room looking impatiently around.

"Lord Jackson. Please come in." Flame says with an inquisitive notion. "And Yes I have had a few run-ins with a few of those things."

"Flamel, I like you. You are definitely one of the good ones. I can tell. You see I consider myself a very good judge of character and I need to ask you a favor. Just please know that this is not a demand but yet a truly heart felt request."

"Anything for you Lord Jackson." Flamel says appreciatively.

"You see, I need someone smart enough to not only find a cure, but someone who can help me bring an end to this chaos."

Flamel nervously clears his throat.

"Are you that man Flamel? Are you able to help me with this?"

"Lord Jackson, I am beyond flattered. I am. But I fear you think to highly of me. I must tell you I have been doing just that since I first came across those things. There were a couple times I even thought I had a cure, yet sadly I came up short on both occasions. You see I just don't know enough about these creatures. There are just too many variables that I don't know. Like what's causing the outbreak. Hell if I knew the origin of how this all started or even what the physical cause is I could possibly find a way to reverse it. And maybe just maybe find a cure or at very least a way to stop it in its tracks."

Lord Jackson starts to chuckle a bit. "I knew you were the right man for the job."

"Lord Jackson, I don't think you quite understood what I was trying to say."

"Oh, I understood Flame, and you know most men would not dare say no to me or simply even admit there short comings. Most men tend to yes me to death trying to hide their inadequacies. Not you though. You spoke the truth" Lord Jackson begins to smile. "Yet, you see it's not what you said that leads me to my conclusion Flamel it's what you didn't say that tells me you are absolutely the right man for the job."

Lord Jackson brings Flamel over to the table in the middle of the room. On that table sits a book upon which Lord Jackson opens for Flamel to read. "And this here is why. My father states this was all a giant miss understanding an accident shall we say. He states it was not his intent and that his intent was to create something better. He called it a longer food source." Lord Jackson chuckles. "Instead he commissioned the creation, the existence of these things, these creatures. And it's all here. It is all right here in this book."

Flamel's jaw drops to the floor. Without a word he dives right in.

"Lord Jackson, this just might work. Give me some time and let me see what I can do. So you know, I will need some test subjects. Living breathing test subjects if at all possible."

"I will definitely see what I can do. But before I do I must ask. What is with this potion of yours? How does one come across such an amazing creation?"

Flamel closes the book and looks at Lord Jackson. He walks over to his things in the corner of the room. He opens his trunk and reaches into a secret compartment and pulls out a small 8oz bottle.

"I dedicated my life to being the best alchemist I can be and to the pursuit of creation. For nothing would bring me closer to god than to create as matter at my will. And as many men before me I thought to myself what is the most precious, the most amazing thing that I could create? Gold. Right?"

Lord Jackson nods his head in agreement.

Flamel continues. "So I dedicated my life to the pursuit that most men only see as crazy or impossible. But Lord Jackson as you have seen with your own eyes, I did it. I have been closer to god than any other man to ever walk this earth. And I am afraid to admit that kind of power comes with a hefty price my friend, a hefty price." Flamel starts to look distraught and a tear starts to fall down his cheek.

Lord Jackson with a true concern grabs Flamel's shoulder. "It's OK. We are all family here. Please, you can tell me."

"Well for one the ingredients. They are not only hard to come by, but they are quite dangerous as well. So being the cautious one that I am I hired an assistant. His name was Jason. He was young and eager to help with anything he could. Such a kind soul.

Now on this particular night I knew I had finally got something. My calculations and my theories were sound. Everything just added up so perfectly. I had no doubt that this was it. The only thing I wasn't sure of was the potency so I took the ingredients and made as much as I could. Know believe it or not with all that I had it only filled two of these bottles right here."

Lord Jackson gently reaches to grab the bottle from Flamel to get a closer look and Flamel pulls it far from Lord Jacksons reach.

"So there is a second bottle?"

"To test a theory I had, that only royal blood had the key component to making this work, I took blood from one of my slaves and tested the elixir. And there was nothing. Then I had him ingest it orally. And still nothing. He didn't even get sick. At that point I had an idea, yet even to this day I can't remember what that idea was.

I know I had told my assistant to bring me the bottle, and as good an assistant as he was, kind, and generous. He could be quite clumsy at times, and this time was no exception. The bottle somehow got away from his grasp and fell to the floor going everywhere. He right away bent down to clean it up. He must have cut himself picking up the glass, cause at just that moment just a drop of the elixir must have gotten into his blood stream."

Flamel puts his hand over his mouth and takes a moment to compose himself. He grabs a stool and sits down. Lord Jackson is enthralled.

"The whole thing only took a few minutes, but it felt so much longer. Hearing his screams, feeling his agony, and seeing what I saw was something I never want to experience again." Flamel sees the curious look in Lord Jackson's eyes. "You see, the elixir as it mixed with his blood. Yes, he was of a royal blood line. It seeped into every pore and every cell in his body started to turn. He went from being an amazing soul to solid gold in a matter of minutes. There was no stopping it. There was nothing I could do." Flamel starts to cry into his hands.

Lord Jackson holds Flamel close as he

weeps.

"I still hear his cries at night when I sleep."

"There, there. It was an accident. It wasn't your fault." Lord Jackson feels the loss Flamel is feeling. "You must have really loved him, huh?"

Flamel wipes his eyes and looks at Lord Jackson. "That I did." Flamel says as he sits up a bit.

"I know." Lord Jackson says.

Flamel holds the bottle out for Lord Jackson to see. "This here is the last and only bottle I have left of what I once considered my livelihood. Yet it is a constant painful reminder of what I have lost, and what I may never have again."

Flamel can feel Lord Jackson's intense draw towards the elixir. Not sure of the intent he has with wanting it as he does Flamel puts it back into the secret compartment from which it came, and starts to walk Lord Jackson to the door.

"Well its getting late, and I want to get an early start tomorrow. I think you're right by the way. If there is a cure to this mess I will find it. Have no fear. Have a good night."

Lord Jackson lost in thought gives Flamel a smile and nods his head. He hears the door lock behind him as he walks down the hallway.

30

There is a fire pit crackling in the midst of a group of musicians. They start to play there instruments as the fire warms their faces, and they begin to sing a song of triumph. A tale of magic, adventure, love, and merriment. Sang with such harmony it warms the hearts of everyone in the courtyard. There is a drink in every hand and a smile on every face. The night is in full swing.

Killian and Emma are off in a quiet corner holding each other close, talking, laughing, and looking deep into each other's eyes. Killian whispers something into her ear, they giggle a bit, and they start to kiss.

Godwin, Edwin, and Sarah chat near the fire with ale in their hands. Edwin raises his goblet in the air to suggest a toast. Godwin and Sarah follow suit.

"A toast." Edwin says aloud. "Raise your glasses high for..." before Edwin finishes his toast he smacks Godwin in the balls causing Godwin to double over spilling his ale. Both Edwin and Sarah burst into laughter.

In the midst of Sarah's laughter she catches a glimpse of Lord Jackson sitting by himself away from the crowd. She can immediately see the worry on his face. She catches a glance and she quickly smiles and winks in his direction. He smiles back but only for a slight moment as his face goes right back to its original worried state.

As everyone is up celebrating Lord Jackson feels uncomfortable and a bit uneasy. He understands that the people need to see life isn't over and that it's important to celebrate these times of triumph over death. He just doesn't feel he can rest and have peace within himself until it's truly over. There is still too much to do.

As Lord Jackson sits mulling over his thoughts an older gentlemen walks over to him.

"My Lord, do you mind if I rest my weary bones next to you? It has been quite a long day."

"Please," Lord Jackson responds. "Feel free. My home is your home."

"That is very kind of you my Lord." The old man replies as he sits. "I hope I am not intruding here but you seem to have a lot on your mind. Would you like a snack?" he says as he rolls up his sleeve and raises his wrist towards Lord Jackson's mouth.

"That is very kind of you, but no. I am

fine."

Lord Jackson leans in a bit closer to the old man. "Though, if you don't mind me asking. Where are you from? You have a very unique sent. I don't quite recognize it."

The old man nervously giggles. "I hail from Spain my lord. The land of love and beauty. A land were the women are as spicy as they are enchanting."

"I am curious then. What brings you this far from home? What is so enticing about our neck of the woods that would have you so far from your family? Surely you must have a family that misses you. Yes?"

"Well my lord, it's actually the other way around. It is I who misses my family. You see, my family fell to this disease about five years ago. My wife, my kids all feel to this horrible disease. I... I..." The old man wipes a tear from his face. "I had to do the unthinkable. I hope and pray that one day I will be able to see them again". The old man tries to pull himself together a bit. "I was not able to bare the pain of living in a home that was just a constant reminder of what I had lost. So I left."

"I don't understand." Lord Jackson responds "Did you say five years ago? I wasn't aware the disease has been around that long."

"Forgive me my Lord, but maybe it didn't reach this area till recently, but I would not lie about my family in that regard."

"Of course, my apologies I did not mean to imply anything of the sort I was just caught off-guard."

At that moment Lord Jackson is reminded of a trip his father went on about five years ago. He remembers distinctly that he begged his father if he could go with and his father strictly forbid it. It hit Lord Jackson that his father must have known about this he whole time and yet he decided to keep putting people in danger anyways.

"That son of a bitch!" Lord Jackson screams out as he stands up. He tossed his ale to the ground as he storms off.

Sarah sees the outburst and walks over to the old man. "What was all that about?"

"I honestly have no clue." The old man says as he looks upon her with worry and a bit of a shiver to his hands.

Sarah, without even a glance at the old man grabs his hand to calm him down. As she stares out to see where Lord Jackson might have gone she tells the old man "Have no fear, I am sure everything will be OK."

The old man felt calmer at that moment than he has ever felt in his life. He truly had no worries. He looks up at Sarah with a grin across his face stretching from ear to ear.

At that moment Sarah let go of the old man's hand and starts to head toward the castle to follow Lord Jackson. His trail was not hard to track and she caught up with him quite quickly.

Sarah places her hand on his shoulder. "What is going on with you? What was that out there?"

Lord Jackson stopping in his tacks turns

and looks at Sarah. A slight look of defeat was a wash all over his face. “That son of a bitch knew this whole time! Five years ago Sarah! Five years ago he tested it ...”

Lord Jackson grabs Sarah and quickly pulls her into an empty room. They can hear the laughter and the fun being had just outside. He closes the window and pulls Sarah to a quiet corner.

“My Father the Prince went on a trip five years ago. And I remember having a strange feeling back then about it because it was the first time he wouldn’t let me join him. He always wanted me to join him cause ‘every trip was a great learning experience’ he would always tell me that. And now I know why. He was testing it and infecting people, even back then. He lied to me, He lied to us. He said he had no knowledge of this but, he has known for at least five years. Maybe even more. Who knows?”

Sarah eases Lord Jackson into a chair forcing him to sit. Holding his hand she sits next to him. They hear the crackling of a fire lightly burning in the fireplace few feet away on the left.

Lord Jackson trying to continue his thoughts, barks out “He is a monster Sarah!”

Sarah rubs the back of his hand and looks him in the eyes.

Now in a very somber manner he continues “He has to be stopped.”

Sarah interjects as she tries to calm him down “He is your father and our prince. Not to mention he is royal blood. And we all know blood is not to harm blood."

Lord Jackson tired of the coddling pulls his hand away from Sarah's.

"Don't be naïve, it happens all the time. Wars are nothing but blood killing blood."

"You know that is not how the King will see it." Sarah says firmly. "I know you and I know what you're thinking of doing. What is going to happen if they decide to banish you or yet worse kill you for it?"

"I don't care what they do to me. Greater men have died for less, and he needs to be stopped. He cannot just get away with what he has done. He just can't"

Sarah sits up straight "Fine, I'm in. What's the plan? What do we do?

"Now wait just a moment. I'm not going to let you ruin your life as well. This is my fight and I won't have you..." Lord Jackson pauses as he sees the look on Sarah's face.

Sarah's face has turned very stern and un-empathetic. And he can feel daggers shoot thru her eyes as he changes his course of thought.

"Fine." He continues. "We will end this together. I was speaking to Flamel earlier and he told me a story of how..."

31

The next morning Sarah looks at Lord Jackson with concern. She notices he looks a bit on the weak side. "When was the last time you ate?" she asks him.

She starts to roll up her sleeve purely out of habit. Then stops when she realizes she simply can't do that for him anymore. It shocks her for a slight moment when she realizes a bit of jealousy has shot thru her body. She grins to herself then quickly snaps back.

She looks deeply into Lord Jackson's eyes as she begs him "Promise me you will feed tonight. I don't care with who. Just make sure you feed. You need to be at full capacity if we are going to do this."

Lord Jackson chuckles a bit and responds. "OK, fine."

Sarah heads downstairs to bring Flamel some breakfast. She reaches his door with a tray of pastries and fruit. She knocks on the door to the laboratory where Flamel has been working nonstop all night and can surely use a break.

"Who's there?" Flamel yells from behind the door.

"It's Sarah," she replies. "I have brought you some food I thought you would be..."

"Please come in." Flamel say quickly opening the door and cutting her off before she could finish her sentence.

With a glance at the plater Sarah holds in her hand Flamel begins to grin from ear to ear. He fills his hands with food as if it was years since he last ate.

"Thank you! Such an angel you are." He says with a mouth full of food.

"My pleasure," she says as she places the plater on the desk. "And please enjoy. I must say though, my kindness this morning has come with slight selfish intensions."

Flamel's eyebrows raise with inquisitiveness.

Sarah grabs a pastry and takes a small bite. "You see, I am quite new to all this and I was hoping we could talk." She explains.

"Well I could use a nice distraction to help clear my mind and any distraction as pretty as yourself is always welcome."

"Do you mind if we go somewhere a little cozier? This room just gives me an uneasy feeling." She asks as she bats her eyes.

"Of course." Flamel replies "I know the

perfect spot." Flamel clears his throat.

Sarah grabs his arm as they walk towards the door and as they get to the door Sarah stops.

"Oh wait!" Sarah says as she goes and grabs the plater of food. She hands the platter to Flamel as she pushes him out the door closing the door behind her. She proceeds to grab Flamel's arm as they walk.

The two of them walk up the stairs to the top of a battlement were they can look out upon the vast country side. Here are a few crates along the wall so Flamel places the plater of food down upon one and sits on another. Sarah stands with her arms resting on the wall as she enjoys the view.

"This is amazing up here. The view is breathtaking. Do you come up here often?"

"I come up here every night to unwind a bit. It helps clear my head. When I first got here Godwin showed me around and brought me up here." Flamel starts to chuckle to himself, "He told me many a fair maiden have succumbed to his..."

Flamel realizing he is in the company of a lady starts to blush.

"So sorry Milady. I lost my manners for a moment."

"It is quite alright. I have been around a lot worse talk." She giggles. "Most of the time the boys forget I am a lady. So I thank you for being so gentlemanly."

The sun starts to break thru the clouds a bit getting a little bit brighter. Sarah puts her hood up and goes to sit. The crate she sits on is in a bit of shade.

Flamel drags his crate over so he can sit closer to Sarah.

"So, what's on your mind? I see you are a bit sensitive to the light. A little bit more than most people I know."

"Yes it seems I am. As you know I am new to this whole thing and even though I grew up around it all. Actually being a part of it is quite different. Now so much of it was already explained to me by Lilith, but there is so much to grasp between explanation and experience."

"Wait, did you say you spoke to Lilith?"

"Well yes, when I was going thru my transformation she came to me in what felt like a dream. She sat me down and she explained so much. Yet actually experiencing it presents question after question. Like why am I so sensitive to the sun when others are not?"

Flamel with a dumbfounded look upon his face now has questions of his own.

"I apologize but, I can't get past this... you actually spoke to Lilith! That is amazing! I have never met anyone who has actually spoken to her before. What did she say? What did you talk about?"

Sarah, a bit confused, takes her hood down for the moment.

"I thought everyone speaks to her when they go thru the change. Are you saying that you have never spoken to her at all?"

"Let me put it this way. In the past 230 plus years that I have been roaming this land of ours, I have never met anyone who has claimed to have spoken to Lilith. Not to mention seen her as well. So please tell me everything."

Sarah starts to tell Flamel everything just as she remembers. She goes into how vividly she remembers flying over a field and seeing Lilith from a distance yet being able to hear her so clearly as if she was right next to her. She tells him all about the room she was in as Lilith introduced her to something called coffee. She tells Flamel all she was able to remember, which leaves Flamel's jaw wide open. With just enough time for a fly to go straight into his mouth. Franticly he spits it out before he chokes.

Sarah chuckles as she slaps him on the back a few times. Flamel attempts to speak once he calms.

"That is truly an amazing gift. Sarah, I feel you just might be the key to our survival. You have obviously been chosen by Lilith herself. Handpicked to lead us to our next stage in life. She sees greatness in you as do I."

Sarah squirms back a bit putting her hood back up. "I don't know about all that."

"You don't have to know about it. You just have to be, and fate will do the rest."

Flamel stands up holding out his hand. Sarah grabs ahold as she stands, and they walk back down together.

"Flamel, you have been an utter gentleman. And I thank you for taking the time to talking with me. I feel so much better."

Flamel blushes and replies. "Please, it is

me who should be thanking you. It has been an eye opening conversation and probably the best distraction I could have ever asked for. Yet sadly I must now get back to my work. The world needs saving and I must play my part."

Flamel as they reach the door to the laboratory pulls Sarah's had to his lips for a quick kiss. "Till next time. It was truly a pleasure."

"The pleasure was all mine."

Sarah turns and walks down the hall as Flamel closes the door. When she reaches the top of the stairs heading back to Lord Jackson's room she hears someone whisper from behind.

"Oh the pleasure was all mine." Said in a mocking female tone.

Sarah turns quickly recognizing Lord Jackson's poor attempt to scare her, and she smacks him in the chest. She fiercely stares daggers at him and continues to walk towards the room.

"Did you get it?" she asks sternly.

"Of course I did. I am as quick and nimble as a cat." He says as he dances nimbly around her holding a bottle in his hands.

"You better have, I provided you with way more time than what was needed." She snarls as she wipes the back of her hand on her dress.

Lord Jackson continues to tease her as he shuts the door to the room behind them.

32

The next morning Jacob is in the kitchen preparing breakfast as he normally does knowing everyone will need there nourishment from celebrating too hard the night before as they normally do. He finely chops some vegetables and mixes them in with the scrambled eggs. He likes to use a nice mix of red and yellow bell peppers, along with some mushrooms, onions, and some diced potatoes. Once everything is cooked and well mixed together he dumps it into a nice serving bowl and places it next to the three loafs of bread he had made earlier.

He looks upon his breakfast spread with his chest held high. Plenty of fruits, meats, breads, and eggs to feed an army, or just a group of refugees trying to stay safe from the evils they have seen beyond the safety of the walls that bind them together. His stare of amazement changes quickly when he hears a scream in the distance. He slowly inches toward the door to the hallway. Loud steps are heard running up the stairs.

"Lord Jackson! Has anyone seen Lord Jackson?" Flamel franticly screams from the hallway. "Please, has anyone seen Lord Jackson?"

Jacob peeks his head out from the kitchen to see Flamel in a panic going up and down the hallway.

"My lord, is everything OK? You look... worried."

Flamel stops dead in his tracks and turns to Jacob. "Jacob my boy Please, tell me you have seen Lord Jackson. Please Jacob tell me you know where he is!"

"I apologize my lord but no I have not. Would you like me to run and check his room?" Jacob replies as he attempts to pull Flamel into the kitchen,

"Please rest a moment. Feel free to help yourself to the food there is plenty. I will run and check his room." Flamel sits sluggishly and puts his head in his hands "No need. I have checked his room twice. He is not there. He is nowhere to be found."

Jacob quickly starts to make a plate of food for Flamel. He scoops some eggs, grabs some fruit, and bread. As he starts to bring it to Flamel. Flamel, head still in hand, points at the eggs. Jacob stops smiles and scoops more eggs on the plate.

"My lord, I am going to check the stables and around the grounds to see if I can find him. I will be right back." he says as he hands the plate to Flamel.

"You just stay right her, OK?"

Flamel nods his head as he shovels the food into his mouth, and Jacob runs out of the room almost running down Godwin.

"Slow down there champ." Godwin says as he makes his way into the kitchen. "Good morning Flamel. Damn it smells good in here. That boy sure can cook I tell you!" Godwin starts to fill a plate for himself. Flamel takes a break from filling his face to ask Godwin. "I know this is a long shot but have you by any chance seen Lord Jackson this morning?"

"No, he is probably still passed out in his room like I should be. And will be once I finish this plate. OK maybe after my next plate." Godwin says as he chuckles to himself.

Flamel puts his unfinished plate down in despair, and places his head back into his hands. This is not completely unnoticed by Godwin. Though he fights the urge to inquire what's bothering him Godwin simply can't hold his tongue. His gut knows something is not right.

"Flamel, what is going on with you my friend? You seem down about something?

As Flamel opens his mouth to tell Godwin what he is worried about Jacob bursts into the kitchen.

"My lord, I looked everywhere I could think of but, Lord Jackson is nowhere to be found." Jacob exclaims.

Flamel slams his fist on the table in an outburst that causes his plate of food to go flying into the air. It also causes Jacob to jump back. Godwin tries to hold back a laugh.

"But," Jacob continues. "I was able to talk to Maria one of the new maidens taking care of the garden who showed me the new peppers they planted. Let me tell you they look so amazing I can't wait to see how they taste."

Flamel impatiently bursts out "Focus Jacob, did she say anything about where Lord Jackson is?"

Jacob slightly startled continues "Oh right, Sorry. Maria told me she witnessed both Lord Jackson and Sarah go out for a ride early this morning."
"Damn it! I knew it! I knew it!" Flamel bursts out again. Godwin grabs Flamel by the shoulder. Both Godwin and Jacob look at Flamel inquisitively. Jacob grabs a glass of water and hands it to Flamel.

"He took it, I told him the consequences and he took it anyways. I should have seen it, but I didn't think he would. But he did. He took it."

"Hey!" Godwin says as he gently smacks Flamel in the back of the head. "Stop it! You are babbling and making absolutely no sense. Now take a deep breath and let's start from the beginning. What's going on?"

Godwin and Jacob both pull up stools. Flamel takes the deep breath Godwin suggests, and begins to calm down.

"The other night lord Jackson came to me. He was asking me about how my elixir works. I told him how I stumbled across its ability, and he took that knowledge along with the elixir and now I fear he is going to do something hasty. Possibly something stupid and dangerous."

"Well that doesn't sound like Lord Jackson at all. And when you say elixir are you referring to the stuff you made the gold with?" Flamel nods as Godwin continues. "Maybe he just borrowed it to make some gold armor."

"Gold armor?" Jacob chimes in with a very confused look on his face." "OK, maybe not gold armor, but I will say this if Lord Jackson did borrow the elixir you can count on it being for something important."

"That is what I am afraid of." Flamel replies. "When we were talking he was going on and on about his theory of who was responsible, how this was all started, and how he needed to put an end to it all. He even showed me the books that were kept notating the process that was used so I could work on a cure. I tried to warn him of the consequences it would have if his mind proceeded down that course. Now I fear he is on his way to do something he might not be able to come back from."

Worried for his friend, Godwin asks. "What has he gone to do?"

Flamel with a broken hearted reply, "He has gone to kill his father."

"This can't be true." Jacob proclaims. "Lord Jackson would never."

"Not to mention the king would have his head." Godwin adds. "Besides why would he need your elixir for that? What is he going to do? Make him drown in gold?"

Flamel nervously smirks. "Well that's not too far off. You see, it is not that he is going to drown in gold. It's that with the use of my elixir, he is going to be turned into gold."

Jacobs eye almost pop out of his head. "Fuck me. It can do that!"

33

Godwin and Jacob gather Edwin, Kilian, and Emma into the kitchen and bring them up to speed. They are all shocked and appalled at the idea that Lord Jackson could even be able to do such a thing.

Edwin is the first to chime in. “We have to get to him now, and talk some sense into him.”

“And what if he doesn’t listen?” Emma questions.

“Then we tie him down until he does.” Edwin continues. “They apparently have a full day’s ride ahead of us, but I think I know how we can get to Calais before they do. Maybe we can stop them before they even walk thru the gates.”

“Perfect,” Godwin jumps in. “We are going to need plenty of water and food, feed, tents, my lute, three horses and...”

"Wait a minute why only three horses? There are six of us here." Emma bursts out.

"That's because only three of us are going." Godwin replies. "This is a man's job, and we don't have time to baby sit."

Emma's head is about to burst with anger, "Baby sit!? Man's Job!? Let me tell you something. I sat back last time because I saw how I was needed here. But I swear I will not be left behind again. I am not leaving my man's side!" she states as she pulls Kilian in close. "And another thing. I thought we needed to get there fast. When I used to go out and get supplies for the tavern I had to learn to be quick. I was the only one there to run the tavern so if I wasn't there I didn't make money. So if you plan on adding some speed to our trip then we cannot carry anything we do not absolutely need. The lighter the better."

"I agree!" Edwin says. "And don't worry the only people that are staying behind are Flamel and Jacob." Jacob looks down in disappointment.

"Someone needs to keep these people fed." Edwin tells him.

"I agree as well" Kilian chimes in as he looks at his angelic Emma.

"Agreed!" everyone else adds with the exception of Godwin.

Edwin looks at Godwin and smacks him in the balls with the back of his hand.

"OK, OK agreed!" Godwin groans. Edwin tries to explain the route they are going to be taking as quickly as he can. Once he feels they all understand it the four of them head out.

As they are saddling there horses Emma looks over at Godwin who has his lute strapped to his back. And she throws him a dirty look.

Godwin just shrugs and smirks. Then as he rides past he sticks his tongue out at her making a funny face. Emma desperately hides a chuckle.

Jacob is perched on the wall above as the four of them ride out of the gate as fast as they can. He sits there a moment watching as they ride off into the distance. Once they are no longer to be seen he lets out his breath, begins to breath, and walks back into the castle.

Bright and early the next morning Jacob is woken from a sound sleep by a rooster just outside his window. The sun rises oh so gently and the light comes creeping in and brushes across his face. He eases his eyes open and starts to yawn as he stretches and rises to his feet. Jacob gets dressed and heads to the kitchen to start his morning routine. As he walks in, before he can even light the stove, he hears something that resembles a loud baby screaming. It sounded as if it was coming from the stairwell. He walks over to the stairwell to see if he hears it again. Maybe if he waits a moment he can hear where it's coming from. At this hour he is used to being the only one awake.

Jacob listens intently but instead of hearing a scream this time he hears some kind of clatter come from down the stairs. He goes to investigate the commotion. The stairs lead to Flamel's laboratory. He knocks on the door and waits for a response. As he is standing there he realizes he doesn't hear anything. Everything is quite. He places his ear against the door.

"Flamel?" Jacob whispers thru the door. "Is everything OK in there?" There is no answer. "Flamel?" he says a little louder.

There is a thud against the door that causes the door to rattle. Jacob jumps back a bit. Startled and shaken up he hears the door unlock but remain closed. Reluctantly Jacob opens the door slowly. There is something wedged behind the door making it impossible to open all the way so Jacob squeezes himself thru the crack of the door into the room.

"Jacob my boy!" Flamel says in a loud whisper from across the room. "Come in! Come in! I think I have it. I think this is it." Flamel says softly, as if the words he spoke where so delicate they would vanish if they were spoken to loudly.

"What is it?" Jacob asks. He looks behind the door to see what was blocking him from entering, and sees a jester crying and urging him to be quite. Jacob rubs his eyes and takes a second look to see the jester was gone and nothing was behind the door.

"The cure. I think I found the cure!" Flamel proclaims.

Jacobs's eyes widen as his grin finds each cheek. He is so overcome with joy and happiness it brings a single tear to his eye.

"Really?" Jacob asks. "A cure?"

"Come, bare whiteness and see for

yourself." He says as he removes a tarp from one of the cages.

Jacob sees a man on his hands and knees breathing heavily. The man looks up at him with a confused look on his face. The man is completely covered in sweet and looks exhausted.

In complete shock the man starts to speak directly to Jacob. "Kind boy, where am I?" the man's voice is quite weak. "Why am I in this cage? Did I do something wrong? Am I being punished?"

Jacob looks at Flamel with shock. Flamel returns the same look at Jacob and walks over to the cage. The man in the cage sees Flamel come closer.

"Nothing of the sort my good man. You had actually fallen ill and just as a precaution we placed you in a safe and secure place. For your safety and for the safety of others." Flamel explains.

"Safety of others? Did I hurt somebody?" the man asks.

"Let's not focus on the past right now. Let us focus on your recovery. Do you know your name?"

The man takes a moment to think. His face gets more and more distraught the longer he thinks about it. "No, I can't seem to remember what my name is. As a matter of fact I can't remember much more than opening my eyes a moment ago and finding myself in this cage."

"Interesting." Flamel says aloud. He quickly walks over to the desk and starts to write down notes.

Jacob walks over to a set of keys on the wall. They rattle as he starts to take them down off the wall. Flamel hears this and quickly walks over to Jacob. He put his hand on Jacobs shoulder to stop him from walking towards the cage with the keys.

"Boy, what do you think you are doing?" Flamel quietly questions the boy. He gently takes the keys from his hand and places them back on the wall.

"I just thought that since he was better I would let him out. That's all.

Flamel leads Jacob to the other side of the room away from the cage. He leans down in front of Jacob to get face to face with him.

Flamel whispers, "Just because he looks better doesn't necessarily mean he is completely cured. There are still quite a bit of testing I need to conduct to make sure he is going to be OK. We don't want to let him loose if he is just going to relapse and turn back into one of those things. Do you understand what I am telling you?"

"Yes." Jacob replies. "I should get back to the kitchen. I can bring you down some food when it's ready? Should I bring some for him as well?"

"Are there any of those muffins left over from yesterday?" Flamel inquires.

"I believe so." Jacob says as he heads to the door. On his way out he takes one more look at the guy in the cage and he thinks to himself that this guy doesn't look as if he could ever hurt a fly not to mention an actual person. He's just sitting in the cage with his legs crossed and his head in his hands. He looks as if he needs a good meal. And that is just what Jacob is going to bring him.

Jacob wakes in his bed. He looks around his room with confusion. He can't believe that everything he was just doing was all a dream. Jacob shakes it off, gets dressed, and heads to the kitchen to start his morning routine. As he walks in, before he can even light the stove, he hears a rooster crow. He starts to think what if it wasn't just a dream but a premonition and his chest puffs up with hope.

While up in the kitchen Jacob makes a breakfast fit for a king. He is so excited at the idea that Flamel just might have made a cure he made enough food to feed the whole castle twice over. He fills two big plates of food to bring to Flamel and the man in the cage and then begins to ring the meal bell.

With a plate in each hand Jacob makes his way downstairs. As he reaches the room he notices the door is partially open. So he cautiously walks into the room. He sees that the room is in shambles and he starts to get nervous. His hands start to tremble as he is still holding both plates of food. He walks carefully over broken glass on the floor to place the plates on the desk. As he sets them down he notices the cage door is now wide open and the man is no longer inside of it.

Jacob takes a slow look around. He sees papers scattered all about, broken glass, and the ink bottle was turned over on the desk where the ink has spelled out on to the floor. From the corner of his eye he sees a silhouette of a man in the corner just standing and facing the wall.

Jacob takes a closer look and quickly determines that the figure is too tall to be Flamel and that it must be the man from the cage. Terrified, he slowly takes a step back to leave the way he came in.

Jacob can feel the glass under his heal as he steps down upon it. He starts to cringe as he hears the crunch it makes. And his eyes widen and his body becomes frozen in fear as he sees this creature quickly turn around and stare him directly in the eyes. He knows right away this is not the same man he was thinking it was. The look in its eyes is one of pure hunger, just not the kind of hunger Jacob was anticipating.

The creature lets out a terrifying scream and a tear falls down Jacobs face. The creature starts to run at Jacob as he feels his bladder release and a warm liquid runs down his legs.

Jacob then feels a hand grab his arm as it pulls Jacob out of paralyzation and snaps him back to reality.

"Run, Jacob run!" Flamel yells as he pulls Jacob thru the door and out to the hallway.

Jacob takes the advice to heart and starts to run as fast as he can. He puts aside all the questions that have built up inside his mind like 'what the hell happened here?' and 'WHAT THE HELL HAPPENED HERE!?' get buried into the back of his head so he can focus on running away. As Jacob runs past him Flamel is able to shut the door but realizes the keys to lock it are still in the room so he starts to run right behind him.

They quickly run down the hall and up the stairs. As they reach the top of the stairs Jacob turns his head to see if the creature is still behind them. He sees the top of the creatures head making its way up the stairs and he starts to run faster. Jacob turns his head back around facing forward and fails to notice an open door which stops him dead in his tracks face first. He smacks into the door so hard he hits the ground and blacks out. Hands from inside the room grab him and pull him in as a second pair of hands closes and locks the door.

Lord Jackson and Sara reach Calais by boat. The boat is a small vessel with barely enough room for the two of them. They are both dressed in tattered cloaks covered from head to toe as not to be seen. As the boat coasts into the dock they feel the sun set behind them. Lord Jackson stands up as the boat reaches the doc, and he reaches down with his hand to make sure the burlap bag that carries what he brought with him was secure to his waist. He places his hand firmly over the sack before he jumps off the boat onto the dock.

Sarah feels the weight of the sun ease from her shoulders as it sets. She removes the hood from her head then grabs the rope at the front of the boat. She jumps onto the dock pulling the boat close and ties it securely to the one of the posts.

Feeling eyes upon her she gradually looks

around trying not to tip off whoever it is that's staring, but she is unable to see who it is. Lord Jackson places Sarah's hood back on her head and his arm around her shoulders. Their faces stay low as they walk thru the port.

A sickly old man who is clearly already half to the wind sitting on an old wooden crate is staring at them as they pass. He grabs an oddly shaped jug from his side and brings it to his lips taking a big swig. He wipes his mouth with his sleeve as he sets the jug down, and he notices the couple he was just looking at are now nowhere to be seen as if they have vanished into thin air. Confused and now wondering if he had really seen them in the first place he begins to wipe his eyes as well.

All the way on the other side of the castle at the front gate two young men arrive on horseback. In a hurry they ride through crowds of people pushing their way thru.

"Out of our way! We need to see the prince!" they yell out franticly. "Out of our way people!"

From the other side of the courtyard Lord Jackson and Sarah hear the commotion. They quickly make their way closer to see what's going on. They see the two men getting off their horses. Lord Jackson tells Sarah that both men look familiar but he can't place where he has seen them before.

"Come with me." Lord Jackson says as he grabs Sarah's hand. "I have an idea."

The two men make their way to a couple of guards. They whisper something in one of the guard's ear and then show them what is inside the bag they have with them. The guard tries to reach in the bag and his hand is quickly slapped away.

"Nay, this here is for the prince's hands only." One of the men says as he clutches the bag tight.

The two men quickly head up to see the prince. As they reach the door to the throne room the two men see two guards standing there motionless. One on each side of the door. The two men look at each other. They quickly make sure one another are presentable. They fix each other's hair and adjust their outfits. They smell each other's breath and then they each take a deep breath in shrugging off there nerves. Then one of the men slaps the other across the face and it is quickly reciprocated by the other. They grab each other by the shoulders and slam their heads together, then they both simply turn and open the door. Without resistance the guards allow them to enter as they hold in there laughter.

The prince is sitting comfortably on his thrown half asleep snacking on some grapes. When he hears the door open and sees two men walk in. He sits up a bit to get a better look at who is approaching. Then he sits back when he realizes it is no one he considers important.

The guards close the door while Prince Edward puts another grape in his mouth and asks the men "Who are you? And why are you here?"

"My lord, I am Steven and this is my brother Benjamin. We have not only brought you a gift but we also have extremely important information that comes with this gift on how it was attained." Steven proclaims to the prince as he hands him the bag he carried in his pocket.

The prince looks inside the bag. "Is this what I think it is?" the prince asks as he pulls out a long piece of gold from the bag. The same piece of gold Flamel made earlier.

"That it is my lord." Benjamin replies with glee.

"Where did you get this?" inquires the prince.

"Well my lord. That is exactly the information we came to tell you." Benjamin began to explain.

"We bore witness to a man who created this out of thin air my lord." Steven chimes in as Benjamin slaps him across the chest.

Benjamin continues "Yes my lord we have seen it with our own eyes."

The prince looks at the two with skepticism.

Steven looks at Benjamin sarcastically as to ask if it was ok for him to speak now and starts to explain. "You see my lord, we were minding our own business when we heard a commotion come from a nearby window. We feared that someone might be hurt so we peeked in to see what was going on."

"Yeah, that's when we saw an older man take blood from a woman while a bunch of others were just standing around watching." Benjamin chimed in causing Steven to slap him across the chest this time.

The two men exchange a few slaps when the prince decides he has had enough and chimes in himself.

"OK, OK, that's enough. Get back to the story already!"

The two men stop immediately. Benjamin nods to Steven to continue the story.

"Yes we saw him take blood from a young woman then he began to mix it with something in a tube. Then he poured whatever was in the tube out onto the table and moments later it turned to gold. It actually turned into what you have in your hands right now. It was the most incredible thing I have ever seen in my life."

"Tell me. Who is this man who can make gold on a whim like this?" the prince starts to demand. "Does this man have a name?"

"I believe his name is Flamel my lord." Benjamin answers.

"It is my lord. His name is Flamel." Steven confirms.

"And where did you witness such an act?" the prince inquired.

"Your castle in England my lord."

"Preposterous! If there was something like that going on there I would have known about it!" the prince proclaims.

Just then a scream is heard for outside the door. It startles both men and they turn their heads toward the noise. While there heads are turned the prince stands and walks up behind them.

"You two have done the right thing bringing this to my attention." The prince says as he puts his arms around them and leads them to the door. After hearing a second scream both men are quite reluctant to leave the room.

"What I am going to need from the two of you," the prince continues. "Is to go back to this Flamel and bring him to me. That way I can witness this miracle for myself." Prince Edward pushes the men out of the door as it shuts behind them.

As Prince Edward turns and heads back to his thrown he suddenly sees Lord Jackson and Sarah standing there. Taken back for a slight moment and not really sure what to make of his sons surprise visit he decides to place the piece of gold into his back pocket so it is out of sight.

"Jackson my boy is that really you?" prince Edward says as he walks closer.

"What they told you was true father." Lord Jackson says with a stern look upon his face. "I have procured the talents of a master alchemist named Flamel to find a cure for this epidemic we are facing. And to prove his worth he showed me how he found the secret to creating gold."

Prince Edward's eyes widen, and his cheeks raise to what could possibly be seen as a grin. He walks straight to his drink station which simply consists of a few goblets and two large carafes one of wine and one of blood.

"Well this is cause for a celebration!" prince says with glee as he pores himself a goblet of blood.

"Sarah?" Prince Edward asks as he gets a closer look. "Is that you? You seem different somehow."

"Yes it is I my lord." Sarah replies.

"Please help yourselves to drinks." Prince Edward offers pointing to his drink station.

"We already have my lord." Sarah replies as Lord Jackson and herself raise two goblets in the air.

"A toast," Lord Jackson starts since the goblets are already in the air.

Screams are getting louder and louder outside, but none of them seem to be fazed. Prince Edward raises his goblet in the air to join them.

"To new discoveries leading us to a new future." Lord Jackson continues.

"To a brighter and richer future, and to family." The prince chimes in.

"To family!" they all say as they clink their goblets together and drink.

"What I am going to need from the two of you is to go back to this Flamel and bring him to me so I can see this miracle for myself." Prince Edward says as he pushes the two men out of the door. The two men stumble forward as the door slams behind them...

Benjamin and Steven look at each other with worry in their eyes as they continue to hear screams in the distance. The screams however seem to be getting louder and fearfully closer with every breath. They hesitantly make their way down stairs.

A woman in tattered rags is tightly clenching a baby to her chest. She coughs as she limps by the two men. Benjamin looks down at his shirt where the woman coughed and noticed he has been soiled by a small spray of blood. He turns to look at the woman and notices her ankle is bleeding as she limps away.

She stops in her tracks to muffle a second cough. She stands there for a moment, quite still, and focuses on an odd spot on the wall in front of her.

Both men are now distracted by the woman and curious as to what on god's green earth could she be looking at so intently that would be preventing her from leaving this havoc filled area. As they both intently scan the wall and see nothing of such caliber they turn back to look at the woman and see her eyes have glazed over, and her breath has increasingly got heavier.

Steven branches out his foot in an unconscious attempt to walk and see if the woman needs help yet his body refuses to move from where he stands. And just then the woman's eyes widen as she looks down into her arms. The baby in her arms who has been surprisingly quiet this whole time is now crying uncontrollably. Yet the sound of the babies cries are dulled by the womanly screams the two men let loose when they see the woman start to bite into her own child's flesh and start to chew.

The two men start to run faster than they have ever ran before. Benjamin vomits in his own mouth. He unsuccessfully tries to stifle it as it sprays out of his mouth and into the air and back into his face and clothes. As a result of having to wipe his face clear enough to see where he is going he falls a few meters behind Steven.

The man in front turns to tell his friend to catch up, and as he does he sees a knight on horseback.

The knight on horseback is Edwin. Edwin and the rest of

the crew have reached Calais just in time to see it has now been overrun by the Plagued. These monsters are everywhere they turn.

Edwin rides up behind Benjamin with his sword drawn. Mistaking him for one of the plagued he swings his sword with a mighty force. In one fluid motion it releases Benjamins head from his shoulders. At this point Godwin who is also on horseback rides up to Steven who seems to be frozen in fear. Godwin grabs him by the collar and throws him onto his horse.

"I've got you sir, don't worry. You're safe now."

Godwin begins to ride away from the chaos, and rides outside the castle walls to a safe remote spot. Steven seems to be catatonic. Godwin dismounts his horse and slowly eases him down to the foot of a nearby tree.

"You will be safe here!" Godwin yells not sure if he can hear him.

Godwin mounts his horse and rides back to the castle. Steven, at the foot of the tree starts to slowly process what has just happened. He places his face in his hand and begins to cry. As the crying begins to be more and more intense he begins to lay on his side in a fetal position.

Flamel sits in front of a fireplace with an axe in his hands. He is telling a story to a room full of youngsters. Six all together including Jacob who is sitting between two beautiful bright eyed girls. They all seem to be around Jacobs age, some a bit older

"So as I pull this very axe out of the plagued creature's head it drops lifeless to the floor. Then I turn to see our young Jacob here also laid out on the ground. That's when these lovely young ladies..." Flamel points to the girls sitting with Jacob "pulled us into the room here. Now we are all safe and sound."

All the youngsters in the room applaud as they smile and ask Flamel to tell the story again. Jacob feeling a bit embarrassed smiles as the two young ladies cuddle a bit closer. The smile dims a bit when he feels his stomach start to grumble.

"Is anyone else hungry?" Jacob asks. "There is a kitchen full of food. Why don't we all go get something to eat?"

They all think that to be a great idea, so they all start heading to the kitchen. Jacob walks up beside Flamel. He tugs at his shirt.

"Want to hear something crazy?" he asks Flamel as they walk.

"OK." Flamel replies.

"I was originally coming down to bring you food because I had a dream you told me that you had found a cure for all this." Jacob giggles as Flamel stays quite. "Isn't that crazy?"

Flamel looks at Jacob with a smirk and a shrug of his shoulders.

"Well," Flamel replies "It might not be that crazy an idea."

"You mean it?" Jacob asks as his eyes widen.

"Well, it's not fully tested yet. As you saw I had a bit of a setback. I do however feel that I am very close."

"Oh, that is such great news!" Jacob says with a smile that reached from ear to ear.

Flamel grabs Jacob by the shoulders to settle him down. He bends over to look directly into Jacobs eyes.

"Jacob you must promise you will not tell a soul. I don't want to get anyone's hopes up. At least not quite yet." Flamel begs of Jacob.

"I promise!" Jacob replies.

Flamel and Jacob walk into the kitchen to join the others. Jacob's two new female friends beckon him to join them. Flamel pats him on the back pushing him in there direction. Jacob looks at Flamel and starts to blush. Flamel smiles then turns to get some food. Jacob makes his way over to the girls who both give him a great big hug. They simultaneously give him a tiny kiss on his cheeks.

Godwin cringes as he reenters the castle to see a woman in tattered rags eating at a baby nestled in her arms. Holding back his own urge to vomit he rides up to the lady and runs his sword into the top of her skull. The woman drops to the ground with the baby still in her hands. Godwin unsure if the baby is still alive mercifully runs his sword thru the baby's heart. Godwin removes a piece of cloth from his pocket and wipes the tears beginning to form from his face just before he wipes the blade of his sword clean.

Godwin catches up to the others as they are all engaged in killing creatures left and right. He rides up to Edwin's side and hears screams of help coming from the nearby pub just on the other side of the courtyard from where they are.

"You take Emma and Killian and see if

you can help whoever is screaming" Edwin calls out to Godwin. "I am going to see if I can find the Prince! Or Lord Jackson, or whoever I see first! God I hope we are not too late!"

"Fine, but if you get into trouble blow this!" Godwin says as he pulls a conch shell from his bag and hands it to Edwin.

Edwin gives Godwin a strange look as he takes it, slowly. Normally this would be followed by some type of snide remark but due to the current time restrictions he refrains.

Edwin makes his way slowly and cautiously up the stairs. Sword drawn and ready to strike as he reaches the top. He peeks his head around the corner before he fully emerges from the stairwell, and sees a creature knelt over and eating at a lifeless body on his left. He sees that the coast is clear to his right, so he sneaks up behind the creature and swiftly lobs off its head.

Edwin looks down the hall to the left and sees two big wooden doors that he assumes is the throne room doors. Normally there would be two guards standing on each side of the doors. Curious as to where the guards might be Edwin then looks down at the creature and its victim and realizes "Oh." There they are.

He walks up to one of the doors and places his ear up against it. He doesn't hear a sound. Exhausted, he places the tip of his sword to the ground to rest his weight. He grips the handle tight. Unsure if the silence is a good sign or a bad one Edwin takes a deep breath in. He exhales and hears a scream come from onside the room.

Edwin immediately jumps back into action and quickly attempts to open the door. The doors won't budge as it seems to be locked from the inside. Edwin stands back from the door he blows the conch shell to call the others. He starts to ram the door with his shoulder. With everything he has he is determined to get that door open no matter what. The door begins to weaken with every slam. The cracks widen and the latch on the inside begins to buckle.

The door finally bursts open and Edwin stumbles in. As he gathers his balance his eyes focus on what seems to be the prince dropped to his knees. Lord Jackson and Sarah both stand there with their hands firmly on their swords, undrawn and not sure what to expect. Edwin stands there silent grasping tightly to the handle of his half drawn sword attempting to make sense of the situation.

Prince Edward is on his knees struggling to breath, grabbing at his throat he lets out an unimaginable scream. He reaches his hand out to Edwin for help and just at that moment his scream that started out with such blood curdling force turned swiftly to a breathless whisper. His trembling body tenses up and freezes in place. His face turns pale and colorless, his body starts to form a shine. He becomes silent and motionless.

Edwin runs up to the prince dropping to his knees. He looks into the prince's eyes just in time to see them glass over with a golden tint. Edwin grabs the prince with both hands and quickly let go. The prince was hard and cold. What was once flesh, was no longer. He was now nothing but a solid piece of gold.

All three, even though they have all just witnessed with their own eyes the impossible event that just took place, stood in disbelief. Sarah grabs Lord Jacksons hand and squeezes. Edwin without taking his eyes off the prince slowly takes a few steps backward. As reality slowly starts to kick back in Edwin suddenly remembers he is not the only person in the room and quickly draws his sword pointing it directly at Lord Jackson.

"Edwin," Lord Jackson says as he draws his sword as well, "What are you doing? It's me!"

"Stand back!" Edwin yells as he stands firm. Unable to make eye contact with Lord Jackson or Sarah. Edwin has his head cocked to the side.

Just then Godwin comes stumbling in. He sees Edwin and Lord Jackson with their swords drawn at each other and he proceeds into the room with caution. Godwin can see that Edwin is shaken up. He walks up to him very slowly and places his hand on Edwin's shoulder.

"Edwin," Godwin begins in almost a whisper, "What's going on brother? Why do you have blades to Lord Jackson?"

"He did it!" Edwin explains. "He..." Edwin points to the prince and gets choked up. "I was too late. I couldn't stop it."

Edwin's glance to the prince causes Godwin to look at the prince which ultimately causes everyone to look at the prince.

"I don't get it." Godwin says. He is a bit confused and not sure what he is looking at. "What did he do?" and at that very moment as the words left his lips Godwin understood. "Oh!" then disbelief kicks in, "No!"

"Yes." Lord Jackson replies.

"Do you mean to tell me, that thing right there at one point in time was once the actual prince?" Godwin asks as he then draws his sword and also points it at Lord Jackson.

Sarah steps in front of Lord Jackson and between the blades. Her breath is heavy and her feet are light. She is more than ready to strike down anyone who dares try and hurt him.

"Everyone relax!" She demands. "We are all on the same team here!"

"No!" proclaims Edwin. "The two of you crossed the line! The line is here and the two of you have clearly crossed said line!" Edwin, with the tip of his sword creates a line on the ground as he speaks. "See, we are here and you ae there! And that is the wrong side of the line!" he screams.

"We did what had to be done, and if you can't see that and want to draw lines! Fine let us draw lines!" Sarah yells as she draws her sword. Her sword was drawn so fast that the tip of her sword reached the tip of Edwin's Adams apple before he could blink.

Edwin takes a slow step back, and he can see Sarah's eyes begin to glow with a red haze. This is also seen by Godwin and he decides to take a giant step back as well.

Lord Jackson tries to ease the situation as he points his sword down toward the ground and places his hand on Sarah's shoulder.

"Everyone please calm down. I do not want to see any of you get hurt. Especially over this. You all know what he has done. He was the sole cause of all this!" Lord Jackson starts to get heated as he points outside to the screams of terror. "He needed to be stopped! He needed to pay for these things that he himself created!"

"He was our Prince! He was your father! Not to mention the Kings son! You can't take justice in our own hands like this! Right or wrong the King alone will have your head for this! And even if we wanted to help you we couldn't because he would have our heads as well! Taking things into your own hands like this makes you no better than he was."

"You're right." Lord Jackson says as he takes his hand and lowers Sarah's blade. "You are absolutely right, and I must accept my fate. I took this all upon myself and should be punished as such. Let Sarah go and I will be at your mercy. A life for a life is only fare."

Lord Jackson takes Edwin's sword and places the tip to his chest, looks Edwin eye to eye, and stipulates. "But you have to be the one to do it."

"Oh just stop it! Why do you have to be so dramatic?" Sarah says as she pulls Lord Jackson back away from Edwin's Sword. "No one is going to die today. You can't."

"Why not? They're right this was all my doing! I need to do the right thing!"

"The right thing doesn't include dying." Sarah says in a soft voice. "I'm pregnant."

Even though the words were soft as they left her mouth, they hit as hard as if they were yelled from mountain tops. A collective exhale is heard in the room as all swords droop waist side.

"Did you say?" Lord Jackson inquires as he tries to wrap his mind around what he just heard.

"Yes. I am Pregnant." She replies sternly with half a smile. Lord Jackson grabs her by the waist and lifts her high in the air turning her about as he laughs in glee.

"Hahaha! I am going to be a father!" He cries out!

"Oh fuck me!" Godwin yells out loud as he drops his sword to the ground. "I never liked the slimy prick of a prince anyway! Come here you two. Congratulations!" he says as the three of them embrace.

Edwin, unmoved by the news, grips the handle of his sword till his knuckles turned white.

"This does not solve anything!" Edwin proclaims in frustration. "This just makes things worse. And fuck you Lord Jackson! I am the one who has to do it!? What kind of selfish bullshit is that? I am supposed to now choose to either kill my best friend that mind you I have known since I was young enough to shit on my own, who is now going to be a father, and would be a great one at that I would say, ..." tears start to trickle down his face "or, allow our community, our way of life to just fall apart turning into chaos because we let you live, not to mention the king will have all of our heads! ALL OF OUR HEADS!"

"Banish us!" Lord Jackson exclaims.

Sarah looks at him with confusion at first but them smiles.

"Yes! We'll leave. We can start over new." Sarah agrees.

"We will leave and never return. You can even tell everyone you killed us if you need. This way you all look like heroes and I get to raise my son." Edwin, visibly contemplating Lord Jackson's scenario looks to Godwin for a bit of affirmation. Godwin nods his head with a smile.

"Besides," Lord Jackson continues. "The King is going to need someone to take control and with all of this gold how could he deny someone of your caliber."

Godwin gives Lord Jackson a look that screams 'what about me'.

"Well there are now two kingdoms, here and home. There is one for each of you."

Godwin walks over to Edwin placing his arm over his shoulder to talk it over. They talk in private for what seems to last a lifetime. Edwin then turns and looks Lord Jackson in the eyes and takes a deep breath.

"You can never come back here ever again. No one can ever know who you are and where you come from." Edwin demands. "We have all been friends for a very long time, but I want to make this very clear. If I see either one of you back here for any reason

I will have to kill you. I love you both, so please do not make me regret this."

Lord Jackson and Edwin embrace.

"I love you too brother." Lord Jackson whispers into Edwin's ear. "You will be missed."

Godwin walks over to a wall where he sees a battle axe displayed. He removes it and walks over to the golden prince. With one big swing he breaks of a nice section of the prince's arm, pics it up from the ground, and walks it over to Sarah.

"Consider this a going away present." Godwin says as Sarah wraps her arms around his neck. She places the golden arm in her satchel.

"Thank you. You are a true friend."

At this point they have all made their way into a giant group hug. Saying their goodbyes to one another. Edwin and Godwin cover Lord Jackson and Sarah in hooded rags and walk them safely down to the marina. Miraculously the boat they arrived in was still there so they climbed aboard.

"Stay strong!" Godwin yells as they wave goodbye.

With heavy hearts Edwin and Godwin both have tears slide down their cheeks as they stand there watching their friends sail away. They know their lives from this point forward will never be the same. Good or bad there will always be something missing. A leader, a brother, a friend.

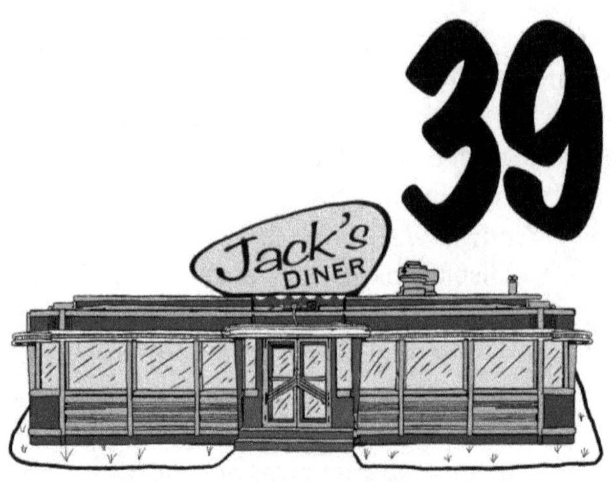

Presently inside the diner, the office door opens. Both Jack and the manager walk out to the front room of the diner. Jack has his arm around the manager's shoulders. The manager is clearly disheveled. The brim of his hairline is matted with sweat. He is slouching as he stands there unable to look anyone on the eyes. He is holding a brown paper bag in his hands gripping it with his life. Jack squeezes his collar bone and grins.

"Can I have everyone's attention?" the manager begins, "I would like you to meet the new proprietor of this fine establishment." He looks at Jack to introduce himself, but jack just nods and squeezes his collar bone even harder. The manager squirms a bit then continues to speak.

"I want you to show him the same respect you have shown me. As for myself I will be taking an early retirement somewhere tropical, and far away from this hell hole that's for sure." He explains as he strokes the paper bag in his hands.

Jack, still with a firm grasp of the manager's collar bone, guides him head first through the front door. Tossing him outside and into the parking lot.

"Enjoy your new shit hole!" the manager yells as he walks away.

Jack turns to address the staff and patrons. He can see everyone is a little on edge from what just happened.

"Ladies and gentlemen, please forgive me the interruption. Have no fear. A tiny bit of housecleaning was in order." Jack says as he looks around seeing everyone is still motionless and possibly scared to move. "As a thank you to you all for your patience and loyalty, your meals will be on the house. Your patronage will always be welcome here at the new and improved Jack's Diner."

A conducive applause of approval is given by the patrons and staff as they all cheer and go on about their day. Jack feels good about his newly found calling in life, and he begins to smile.

Jack, just then feels a tug at his shirt. He turns to see Katie who is possibly smiling bigger than he is. She turns to walk into the kitchen thru the swinging doors. Jack follows. He walks thru the swinging doors and before they stop swinging Katie wraps her arms around his neck. She gives him such a kiss it causes him to loose balance and forces his back against the wall. Her left leg raises with her foot pointing to the sky.

Jacks arms wrap around her body as he kisses her back. Her foot returns to the ground as there embrace loosens.

"Thank you." She says with a whisper.

Jack blushes and smiles. He places his hands on her waist, and he nods his head.

The pick-up bell rings as they hear the cook yell "Order up!" Katie takes a step back unable to break eye contact.

"Looks like my order is up." She says with a twinkle in her eye.

Jack opens the swinging door with his right hand allowing Katie to head back to work. She walks past him with a skip to her step.

At the end of her shift she hears the pick-up bell one last time for the night followed by the inevitable "Order up!" She walks over to the window picking up two plates. One plate consisted of a juicy bacon double cheeseburger with fries as the second had a huge cob salad with a side of ranch dressing. She brings both plates to the counter placing the cob salad in front of Jack, and she wastes no time taking a huge bite out of her bacon double cheeseburger. Jack see's the juices from the burger run down her chin as he plunges his fork into his salad and he just smiles.

The hairs on the back of his neck start to stand up. Then just before he gives it a second thought he locks eyes with Katie. There gaze gets stronger with each bite they take. With his heart racing like a young school boy, he feels his next chapter start to take heed. In fact he is so caught up in the possibilities that lie ahead he fails to hear the sirens about two miles out

that are quickly closing in around them.
Or does he?

The End.

Printed in the USA
CPSIA information can be obtained
at www.ICGtesting.com
LVHW010926161223
766605LV00047B/894